ANCIENT CULTURE AND SOCIETY

THE ROMANS AND THEIR GODS
In the Age of Augustus

ANCIENT CULTURE AND SOCIETY

General Editor
M. I. FINLEY
Professor of Ancient History
at the University of Cambridge

A. W. H. ADKINS Moral Values and Political
Behaviour in Ancient Greece
H. C. BALDRY   The Greek Tragic Theatre
P. A. BRUNT   Social Conflicts in the Roman Republic
M. I. FINLEY   Early Greece:
The Bronze and Archaic Ages
A. H. M. JONES   Augustus
G. E. R. LLOYD   Early Greek Science: Thales to Aristotle
C. MOSSÉ   The Ancient World at Work
R. M. OGILVIE   The Romans and Their Gods
B. H. WARMINGTON   Nero: Reality and Legend

Other titles in preparation

THE ROMANS
AND THEIR GODS
In the Age of Augustus

R. M. OGILVIE

Fellow and Tutor in Classics,
Balliol College,
University of Oxford

W · W · NORTON & COMPANY · INC · NEW YORK

ISBN   0   393   05 399   7

ISBN   0   393   00 543   7

For Tim

CONTENTS

PLATES

*Plates I, II and IV are reproduced by permission
of The Mansell Collection, London, and Plate III
by permission of the Museo Capitolino, Rome.*

PLANS

(*Drawn by Denys Baker*)

PREFACE

I should like to acknowledge the help which I have received from four friends—Dr. M. I. Finley, Mr. C. M. Haworth, Mr. A. J. Saint and the Revd. P. D. King—who have read and criticised this book. The little which I have learnt about the gods of the Roman world I owe entirely to Dr. S. Weinstock.

Errachd   R. M. OGILVIE

Acknowledgements

The author and publishers are grateful to the following for permission to quote from copyright material: Edinburgh University Press for David West: *Reading Horace,* and University of California Press for Cyril Bailey: *Phases in the Religion of Ancient Rome*.

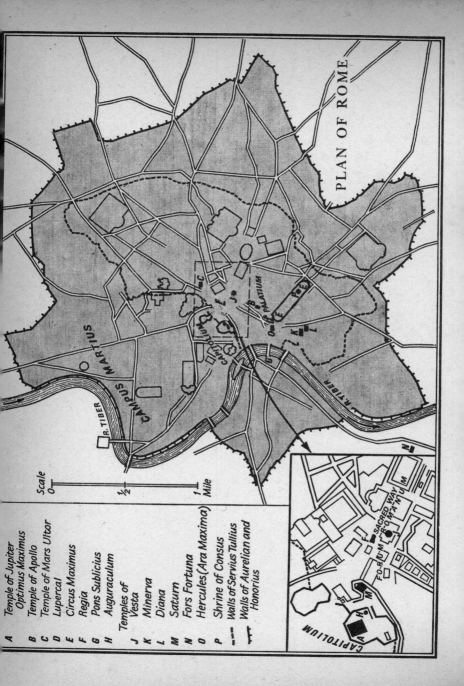

PLAN OF ROME

Scale
0   ½   1 Mile

R. TIBER

CAMPUS MARTIUS

CAPITOLIUM

PALATIUM

R. TIBER

CAPITOLIUM

FORUM ROMANUM

SACRED WAY

A   Temple of Jupiter
     Optimus Maximus
B   Temple of Apollo
C   Temple of Mars Ultor
D   Lupercal
E   Circus Maximus
F   Regia
G   Pons Sublicius
H   Auguraculum
     Temples of
J   Vesta
K   Minerva
L   Diana
M   Saturn
N   Fors Fortuna
O   Hercules (Ara Maxima)
P   Shrine of Consus
- - -   Walls of Servius Tullius
———   Walls of Aurelian and
     Honorius

Introduction

LATIN poetry is studded with the names of gods and Roman works of art, in particular the great public monuments, like the Altar of Peace with its magnificent sculptures dedicated by Augustus in 13 B.C., regularly depict religious scenes. But it is difficult for us to feel that this world of gods and goddesses is more than decoration. The influence of Christian education and tradition is so strong that we cannot imagine that pagan gods ever had any real meaning or that people could actually believe in their existence or their power. Yet, whatever his own personal beliefs may have been, there is no doubt that Augustus hoped to reconstruct Roman society on the foundation of a revived religion and that many of his contemporaries—men like Horace, Tibullus, Virgil and Livy—were genuinely moved by faith. They were able to feel emotionally excited about the traditional stories of the gods, even when, with the rational side of their minds, they would dismiss them as fictions. So if we are to understand the history of the late first century B.C. and of the first century A.D., we must try to get under the skin of the Romans, see how their religion worked and appreciate how they thought about it.

No Augustan writer has left us a spiritual auto-biography or diary which might form the basis of a more general account of the religious life of his age. It has to be built up from inscriptions and documents, and from scraps of evidence from many writers. Since our sources are so limited, I have used evidence from earlier or later periods where it seems reasonable to suppose that the thoughts or ceremonies which they report were also typical of the Augustan age. I have not aimed to give a complete picture but rather to single out the most important features, the features which we meet most often in reading classical authors.

There is a danger in generalising about religion.

1

Christianity is a religion with a doctrine which is taught and with a creed which is accepted by believers. So it is reasonable to expect that there will be a common measure of agreement between Christians about their religion and therefore the beliefs and experience of one Christian can be used in some sense as typical of Christians as a whole. But there was no dogma in Roman religion, no Thirty-Nine Articles or Westminster Confession to which a believer had to subscribe. A Roman was free to think what he liked about the gods; what mattered was what religious action he performed. For a Roman, there was no contradiction when Julius Caesar, as *pontifex maximus*, head of the Roman state religion, and so responsible for several official festivals concerned with the dead, publicly expressed his opinion that 'death was the end of everything human and that there was no place for joy or sorrow hereafter' (Sallust, *Catiline* 51). Such views would be unthinkable in an Archbishop of Canterbury. It would be quite wrong to suppose that a substantial body of Romans would have shared the beliefs outlined in this book: some might have held some of them.

The only sects which had anything approximating to a creed in the Christian sense were the mystery cults which came, largely from the East, to Rome in the course of the late Republic and the early Empire—cults such as those of Isis, Mithras and Sabazius. The cults can be distinguished by the fact that their devotees believed that there were certain mysteries which could only be revealed to those who had been initiated by special ceremonies into an inner circle of worshippers. The initiates formed a closed, almost secret, society. They alone had the key to the understanding of the universe and could communicate with their god. Another common feature of these cults, which sets them apart from Roman religion in general, is that they usually offered the initiates the promise of a better life in the world to come, a promise which appealed most strongly to the poorer and more oppressed elements in Roman society. Yet these 'Oriental' religions were not exclusive. It was possible to be an initiate of Isis and at the same time to continue with the usual worship of the Roman gods: one could even join several mystery religions at once, as a multiple insurance policy. Domitian, who was later to be emperor and to hold all the leading pagan priest-hoods, was an initiate of Isis and was only saved from death in A.D. 69 by the protection of some priests of Isis. But since these 'Oriental' religions are not central to Roman religious tradition, I have not gone into them.

Ancient religion was tolerant and non-sectarian. In this it was unlike ancient philosophy. The adherents of Epicurean and Stoic philosophy fought long and acri-monious feuds, as one can see by reading Lucretius. The reason for this difference between religion and philosophy is that the philosophers maintained various factual propositions about the world—that it was made of 'breath' or atoms, that it was finite or infinite, and so on—whereas ancient religions only presupposed the existence of forces capable of being persuaded by prayer and sacrifice. Since Roman religion offered no dogmas about the universe, there was nothing for people to contradict or to argue about. Philosophers, on the other hand, had elaborate systems which they defended to the last detail with grotesque ingenuity.

There was, however, one religion in the ancient world which was stubbornly exclusive—Judaism (and, later, Christianity). The Jews believed that there was only one God and only one acceptable form of worshipping that God. A Jew who allowed himself to offer sacrifice to any other god thereby compromised himself. The God of the Jews was a jealous god. To recognise the possible exis-tence of other gods was betrayal and apostasy. Hence the Jews always refused to make even the token gesture of acknowledging Roman gods, although it was a gesture which all the other nations of the Roman Empire were prepared to make. It is no wonder that the Jews were so heartily disliked by the Roman authorities. But for long it was not a serious problem; Judaea was a very small country and the Jews in the rest of the Empire belonged to the lowest orders of society. It was only when Christianity,

the successor to Judaism, became, about A.D. 250, a powerful force in the Roman world and absorbed a Greek
philosophical system that bigotry and persecution began
in earnest.

In the first centuries B.C. and A.D. Rome was the capital
city of a huge and motley Empire, which comprised all
sorts of races, religions and colours. In a series of wars
she had conquered most of Europe and the Middle East.
The Celts in Britain, France and Germany had become
as much part of the Roman Empire as the eastern
nations in Syria and Asia Minor who had enjoyed a long
and utterly different culture. In the south the Phoeni-
cian peoples of North Africa had been subdued after the
Punic Wars, and even Egypt, with the oldest civilisation
known, was brought under Roman control in 31 B.C.
The most influential of these subject peoples were the
Greeks with whom the Romans had had very close ties
for over four hundred years and whom they eventually
absorbed in 146 B.C. The Greeks were far more advanced
and original than the Romans, supplying them from
very early times with many of the myths and ideas about
their own gods, so that it is difficult to speak about
'Roman' religion as a separate thing. Roman religion is
essentially the result of the fusion of primitive Latin
and Greek elements.

Under the Roman Empire all the different peoples
continued to speak their own languages, as the events at
Pentecost show so clearly (*Acts* II), and to worship their
own gods in their own way. Yet, at the same time, Rome
managed to impose on them certain common features.
Latin was the common official language. The Roman
form of government was the same everywhere, and the
Romans tended to perpetuate their own religious beliefs
and customs throughout their Empire. They were able
to do this because men went regularly from Rome to run
the provinces and the legions of the Roman army moved
from country to country. It was like the situation which
existed in the British Empire. But Rome itself, which
probably had a population of over a million in A.D. 1,
was a cosmopolitan place which attracted people from

all over the world. One should not think of the Romans as a single, pure race. Seneca consoles Helvia by assuring her that foreigners make up more than half Rome's population (*Consolation* 6): Moorish slaves leading elephants about; fair-haired Germans of the Imperial Guard; Egyptians with shorn heads; a Greek professor, his scrolls in charge of the Nubian at his heels; Oriental princes with coloured impassive suites; wild men from Britain, staring their eyes out. All of these various people will have retained to some extent the religious traditions of their own home-countries, but we know as little about them as we do about the attitudes of the ordinary, un-educated man-in-the-street. Our knowledge of Roman religion is derived from a handful of articulate and highly educated Romans who are representative of only a very small class, a class, moreover, which was brought up to think of everything intellectual in Greek rather than Roman terms. The illiterate mass of the population has left almost no record apart from a few inscriptions; and even these cannot be trusted to give a real insight into their beliefs any more than can the conventional verses which appear in the columns of local newspapers:

> A little flower just lent not given
> To bud on earth and bloom in Heaven.

Nonetheless, when allowance for this has been made, it does seem that concern for religion did go deep into Roman society. Even if they could not explain or justify why they uttered the prayers or performed the cere-monies that they did, most Romans did instinctively believe in their efficacy. Lucretius has left us a vivid portrait of such a person 'seen often with veiled head turning towards a stone, drawing near to every altar, lying prostrate on the ground with outstretched hands, sprinkling the altars with the streaming blood of beasts and linking vow with vow' (*On the nature of things* V, 1198*ff*.). In a similar tone Cicero complains that super-stition is rife: 'Wherever you go, it follows you, whether you listen to a prophet or an omen, whether you sacrifice a victim or catch sight of a bird of warning, whether you

interview an Oriental soothsayer or an Italian diviner,
whether you see lightning or hear thunder' (*On divination* I, 48). Even in the chaotic years of the late Republic
the Romans did not wholly give up their religious
observances. Cicero can write that his countrymen still
surpass all other people in their performance of religious
duties (*On the nature of the gods* II, 8). This picture of
a people who took their traditional religion seriously is
not disproved by individual exceptions. In every age
some of the most highly educated men are apt to be the
most agnostic. Cicero himself was sceptical. Although an
augur, an official priest concerned with interpreting the
will of the gods (p. 56), he expressly denied the possibility of divination. Although for rhetorical effect in a
public speech he attributes his success in unmasking the
Catilinarian conspiracy to the gods (*Against Catiline* III,
22), he does not give them even a breath of credit in his
letters and his more intimate reflections on the events
of 63 B.C. Religion never touched him actively and even
his philosophy was academic, unrelated to the practical
affairs in which his deepest emotions were involved. But
most men were not as detached as Cicero. Sulla carried
round with him wherever he went an image of Apollo
(Plutarch, *Sulla* 29); his great rival, Marius, as Sallust
twice emphasises (*Jugurtha* 63, 1; 90, 1), relied constantly on the gods and was in all things guided by what
he believed to be divine will. If this was true of leading
statesmen, it was presumably still more true of the
common folk. The reaction of the people of Enna in
Sicily may be taken as typical (Cicero, *Against Verres* IV,
114): in all sincerity they believed that Verres' sacrilege
in stealing their statue of Ceres, the goddess of corn, was
the direct cause of a catastrophic crop-failure.

I stress this point because I am convinced that even
under the late Republic, when many temples had fallen
into decay and many priesthoods were left unfilled, the
religious instincts of the people of Italy were strong, and
hence that there was a widespread will to believe in the
gods which only needed some official encouragement and
a favourable climate of opinion to usher in an age of

greatly revived devotion and worship. This is what
happened under Augustus. It was not the result of a
deliberate policy, although Augustus set a conspicuous
example and provided the necessary means for the rebuilding of temples and re-establishing of cults. You
cannot make people believe to order. Perhaps one of the
chief factors was a sense of guilt. A Roman citizen aged
fifty in 30 B.C. would have lived through a generation of
unexampled atrocities and civil wars. We can get some
idea of the passions that were roused in that period and
of the horrors that occurred by reading of what happened to Padua, Livy's home-town, or to the fine city of
Perugia, besieged by Octavian from 41 to 40 B.C. and
burnt to the ground. There was no security of life or
property. While ruthless and ambitious generals com-
peted for power, lesser men were crushed in the process.
Read the pathetic account, preserved by Livy, of how the
elderly Cicero, the greatest ornament of his age, was
dragged out of hiding and butchered, or read in
Plutarch's *Life of Antony* how the Triumvirs cheerfully
proscribed their relations, (as Shakespeare puts it:

Antony These many, then, shall die; their names are
         prick'd.
Octavius Your brother too must die; consent you, Lepidus?
Lepidus I do consent, —
Oct.   Prick him down, Antony.
Lep.   Upon condition Publius shall not live.
         Who is your sister's son, Mark Antony.
                 Julius Caesar IV, 1, 1–6)

and you will understand the fear and suspicion and
degradation of the time. Civilisation seemed to be break-
ing down.

How had this happened? Why had Rome's greatness
disintegrated? It was natural that frightened people
should turn to the gods in their despair and, as they did
so, see a connexion between their present ills and their
past neglect of religion. Sallust put it clearly when he

said that greed had ousted all Rome's good qualities and
taught her instead 'pride, cruelty, neglect of the gods
and total materialism' (*Catiline* 10, 4), and Cicero must
have thought it a point likely to appeal to his audience
when he claimed that 'the gods had sent the civil wars
on the Roman people as a punishment for some offence'
(*For Marcellus* 18). And then, when all hope was almost
gone, Octavian, later to be called Augustus, succeeded in
restoring peace and prosperity to Italy. The relief was
enormous and took the form of gratitude to the gods,
because to men of that generation peace *was* a miracle,
just as war could only be explained by divine anger.
Besides, Octavian, the architect of peace, did not hesitate
to attribute his success to divine assistance. This spirit
rings through Horace's second ode of the first book:

> Our younger generation, or what shreds of them survive
> their fathers' sins, will hear that Romans sharpened
> against Romans the swords which should rather have
> killed our enemies the Persians.
>   What god can the people call on to shore up our top-
> pling Empire? What prayer can the Virgins din into the
> ears of their goddess Vesta who does not listen to their
> chanting? Whom will Jupiter appoint to expiate our
> crimes?[1]

As David West comments (*Reading Horace*, p. 97), 'the
strength of this poem, as of so much of the literature of
the period, lies in its deeply moving sense of the Civil
Wars as a divine retribution for the guilt of Rome, and
in the fervent gratitude' for her delivery.

The civil wars, then, and their end, more than anything else, made men's minds receptive once more to the
call of the old religion. The aim of this book is to show
what that religion was like and how it could claim the
faith of the Augustan age: 'To understand the success of
the Romans,' Dionysius of Halicarnassus, the Greek historian who came to Rome in 30 B.C., wrote, 'you must
understand their piety.'

[1] Lines 21–30: translated by David West.

I

The Gods

MOST people have had the feeling at some point in their lives that they cannot control, or even understand, what happens to them. A friend is killed in a car crash; a plague of snails eats their lettuces but leaves the garden next door unmolested; they never have luck in love; they are faced with the awkward dilemma of jeopardising their career or hurting a friend; try as hard as they will, they cannot cure themselves of telling a lie when they are in a tight spot. These, and a thousand other experiences, not only make them feel helpless but also encourage them to believe that there are powers and forces outside them which are responsible.

It has always been a traditional function of religion, including Christianity, to satisfy these anxieties and to give us a sense of security in a frightening and unpredictable world. The things that happen to us are not blind freaks: they are the direct consequences of what God wants to do with us. In recent centuries the cruder implications of such a doctrine have been progressively eliminated.

Nevertheless, it will help to understand how the Romans thought if we try to recapture these feelings of anxiety, 'alone and afraid, in a world we never made'. For although they had made great strides in a number of practical and administrative fields, they were rarely creative thinkers. They produced no native philosophers or scientists. They were content not to ask fundamental questions about the processes of nature, not to seek scientific explanations, as the Greeks had done, for natural phenomena. They were, of course, keenly alive to the importance of those processes. Harvest, trade, war, pregnancy, health—these were not things to be treated lightly; they were the essential facts of life because on them, as for us today, human happiness depended. They were at once so important, so mysterious and so uncontrollable that the Romans regarded them as supernatural rather than natural processes. They saw the germination and growth of a plant as in itself something supernatural and, whereas we might research into the genetic structure of the plant-cell in order to produce a good crop, they endeavoured to discover means of ensuring that that supernatural process should continue, by conciliating the divine power that was inherent in the process or which controlled it. A scientific law was not an abstraction but a concrete manifestation of divine activity.

A Greek historian, Polybius, one of the most acute observers of the Roman way of life in the second century B.C., summed it up when he wrote: 'Those things of which it is impossible to ascertain the causes may reasonably be attributed to God or Fortune, if no cause can easily be discovered. But where it is possible to discover the causes, remote and immediate, of the event in question, I do not think that we should have recourse to divine agency to explain them' (XXXVII, 9, 2). The Romans found that life worked better for them if they did not look too hard for the causes but acted on the assumption that 'all action is associated with, and the result of, divine or spiritual agency'.

The chief feature, then, of Roman religion was the belief that all the important processes in the world were divinely activated and, conversely, that different gods had charge of particular functions and spheres of activity. Some of the most primitive cults show by their very names how the simple farmers of early Rome were naturally concerned to deify the agricultural operations on which their livelihood depended: Flora, Pomona (fruit), Consus ('The Storer', from *condere*), Robigus (blight), Ceres (growth; cf. *creare*), and so on. There is preserved an ancient list of invocations, derived from the manuals of the priests, which demonstrates again how the gods were thought of in terms of functions: Lua Saturni, Salacia Neptuni, Hora Quirini, Virites Quirini, Maia Volcani, Heries Iunonis, Moles Martis and Nerio Martis (Aulus Gellius XIII, 23). Several of these titles are so obscure and so archaic that their meaning cannot now be recovered, but we can be reasonably certain about the 'Disease-ridding power of Saturn', the 'springiness of Neptune' (as in the gushing of a fountain), the 'growing power of Vulcan' and the 'strength of Mars'. In a world without matches or lighters, fire is precious and Vesta, the goddess of the hearth, was from immemorial times one of the most venerated goddesses, so much so indeed that she never suffered the fate of other functional deities of being clothed with human shape and attributes. In the long evolution from a small farming village into a great commercial and industrial town Rome clung on to the old forms of worship because they had worked but also introduced new ones as new needs, new functions and new activities began to appear in society. An economic slump in the early fifth century, associated with a corn-shortage and serious epidemics (or, possibly, the arrival of malaria) called for the institution of the cult of Mercury for the success of business transactions (495 B.C.), Ceres for the process of growth (496 B.C.) and Apollo for the power of healing (before 450 B.C.).

In this way most of the things which were vital for the well-being of society were thought of as functions of a god or as gods functioning. A house is only as secure as its door: the opening and closing of the door, and the passage of a man from the privacy of his home into the racket of the outside world, and *vice versa*, can be critical events, and, in consequence, they were held to be in the power of a god, Janus. Janus Patulcius opened the door, Janus Clusivius closed it. Whether the opening and closing resulted in good or evil for the person concerned would, therefore, depend on Janus' favour. The divine powers associated with the door itself were even more closely defined: the Christian writer Arnobius, drawing probably on Varro, assures us that Limentinus presided over the threshold, Cardea over the hinges and Forculus over the leaf of the door (*Against the pagans* II, 15, 5). Particularly in a farming community, the sky and the changing pattern of the weather command constant attention. The sun has appeared for the last thousand days: is it certain that it will appear tomorrow? How does it operate and how is it controlled? A drought could ruin a village in Italy then just as much as it can in India today. How is rain rationed? The terrifying and unpredictable flashes of lightning contain huge stores of energy. How are they directed? All the different aspects of the weather could only be understood as activities of a power or powers in the sky—Jupiter Lucetius who controlled the light, Jupiter Fulgur who sent lightning, Jupiter Elicius who regulated rainfall, and so on. Livy tells how the sound of a mysterious voice issuing from the ground at a tense moment in the war with the Gauls was promptly identified as a god—'The Speaker' (Aius Locutius). With poor communications and dangerous roads it would be a rash thing to set out on a journey without having squared 'the god who invented roads and paths' (*C.I.L.* VII, 271).[1]

Gods were presumed as and when the need for them arose, but the multiplication of functional deities could be carried to ridiculous and quite unreal lengths, especially by professional priests with an urge for systematisation and a liking for lists. Fabius Pictor, historian of the late third century B.C., recorded a list of the gods that the *flamen* of Ceres invoked when he performed a sacrifice to Earth and Ceres: 'First Plougher, Second Plougher, Harrower, Sower, Top-dresser, Hoer, Raker, Harvester, Gatherer, Storer, Distributor' (Vervactor, Reparator, Imporcitor, Insitor, Obarator, Occator, Sarritor, Subruncinator, Messor, Convector, Conditor, Promitor: Servius, *On the Georgics of Virgil* I, 21). It is doubtful whether the ordinary farmer really carried his beliefs as far as this, any more than Petronius should be taken quite literally when he describes Trimalchio, the *nouveau-riche* villain of his *Satyricon,* worshipping as family gods Profit, Luck, Gain (Cerdo, Felicio, Lucrio: *Satyricon* 60). Such lists of minor functional spirits— *Indigitamenta,* as they were called—were probably

[1] There are two standard collections of Latin inscriptions: *Corpus Inscriptionum Latinarum* and *Inscriptiones Latinae Selectae* referred to here respectively as *C.I.L.* and *I.L.S.*

theoretical exercises, but some of them do correspond to activities about which people were really worried. A new-born baby is helpless and vulnerable. To keep off harmful spirits, three men came at night with an axe, a pestle and a broom and beat the threshold of the house where it lay. The men, Varro says, represented gods, Intercidona, Pilumnus and Deverra, who controlled the processes of cutting, crushing (?) and sweeping by which evil spirits could be removed. By Augustus' time this ceremony was probably no more than a polite custom, like carrying a bride over the threshold or meeting a dark stranger with a lump of coal at New Year. But it serves to illustrate the underlying idea that important functions are in the hands of gods. As late as A.D. 183 the Arval Brethren were reduced to praying to Getter-down, Breaker-up and Burner (Deferunda, Commolenda, Adolenda) in their attempts to deal with a fig-tree which they had discovered surreptitiously growing on the roof of the temple of Dea Dia.

But function is not confined to physical phenomena like opening doors or producing children or even like the rising and setting of the sun. Many natural objects in themselves provoke the kind of wonder that leads men to think of them as more than natural. In the hot, sunny climate of Italy, a spring of fresh water or a copse of trees inspires grateful respect. The Romans thought of them as sacred places in which a spirit dwelt. In a famous passage of the *Fasti* (III, 295–6), Ovid writes: 'There was a grove below the Aventine dark with the shade of oaks and when you saw it you would say "there is a deity there"', and in exactly similar terms Evander in the *Aeneid* (VIII, 351–2), says of the primeval forest which clothed the Roman Capitol: 'some god (we do not know what god) has this grove for his dwelling'. This is probably a relatively recent idea, for there is no evidence that there was a stage in early Roman religion when men believed in undifferentiated spirits (*numina*) inhabiting woods, springs, rivers, lakes, caves and the like. On the contrary it seems that the function of these places was thought of as supernatural and divine and that this primitive idea was changed—under the influence largely of Greek ideas which thought of gods in human terms—into the idea that they were the residences of gods whose function it was to preside over them.

The elder Pliny writes that 'trees were the temples of spirits and that according to an ancient ritual simple farming communities even now dedicate an outstanding tree to a god. We worship groves and their very silences.' Similarly Servius, the ancient commentator on Virgil, says: 'There is no spring which was not sacred', and there is a host of inscriptions, dedications carved in stone, to bear him out. When Horace wrote his ode to the spring of Bandusia (*Odes* III, 13), it was its religious associations which inspired him quite as much as the fact of its being the ancient equivalent of an iced-water machine on a hot day. If we don't understand that, we cannot begin to appreciate what the spring meant to him or what his poem is about. Lakes and rivers were thought of in the same way. In time most of the big rivers of Italy, such as the Po and the Tiber, developed elaborate cults of their own. 'Father Tiber', who figures prominently in the *Aeneid*, is pictured in art as an old, bearded man rising head and shoulders from his water. Smaller rivers, except for tourist attractions like the Clitumnus so vividly described in a letter written by the younger Pliny (VIII, 8), are not much heard of but were no less venerated. In another letter (VIII, 20), Pliny has a polished account of Lake Vadimo (Bassano), the site of a great battle against the Etruscans in 310 B.C. After mentioning some of its peculiarities he adds that 'there is no boat on it, for it is sacred'.

So far I have referred chiefly to the concern of individuals and families to ensure the continuance of beneficial natural processes, but the activities of groups, whether small professional guilds or large cities, also involve similar processes. In the days before trade-cycles or general elections or social classes had been reduced to exact statistical analysis, groups trusted for their prosperity on the belief that their activities were subject to divine control. Minerva rather than fluctuations of con-

sumer-demand governed the fortunes of most industries:
indeed Phileros in Petronius' novel can refer to a jack-
of-all-trades as a 'man of every Minerva' (*Satyricon* 43, 8).
In a busy commercial town like Ostia each guild worshipped a particular god. The rope-sellers of the har-
bour-town honoured Minerva as their preserver; the
corn-measurers paid special worship to Ceres; Mars was
evidently the patron of the builders. There are remains
of temples associated with guilds which served both as a
meeting-room and as a place for the guild-worship. Not
only merchant-guilds had gods to safeguard their functions. One of the most exciting inscriptions from Roman
Britain is a dedication at York by Scribonius Demetrius,
probably the schoolmaster from Tarsus who accompanied Agricola, governor of Britain from A.D. 78 to 84,
and must have assisted his educational programme
(Tacitus, *Agricola* 21, 2), to 'the gods of the Governor's
residence', functional deities no doubt often invoked in
times of stress by Head-Quarters.

Beyond the small groups stood the community as a
whole with its common needs and its common interests.
Each town had a patron deity who reflected its aspira-
tions and activities and who, in later time, was thought
of as making his home there. Vulcan was such a god at
Ostia. The priest of Vulcan, usually a leading figure in
the town, was responsible not only for the cult of Vulcan
but also for the general religious observances of the town,
which illustrates the pre-eminent position that Vulcan
enjoyed. At Praeneste the role of patron deity was filled
by Fortuna Primigenia, at Falerii by Minerva, at Veii by
Juno who was so effective that the Romans could not
capture Veii until by a ceremonial summons (*evocatio*)
they had persuaded her to resign her function of looking
after the interests of the Veientanes and to migrate to
Rome. The belief that communities were watched over
by particular powers was by no means confined to Italy.
Even in Britain there is a dedication to Brigantia, the
goddess who directed the formidable confederation of
the Brigantes.

By the first century B.C. Jupiter Best and Greatest

(*Optimus Maximus*), in his proud temple that overlooked the heart of the city, had for a long time come to
be regarded by the Romans as their champion, who
ensured their success and gave vigour to all their under-
takings. At the height of the Catilinarian crisis Cicero
proclaimed that it was Jupiter 'who had withstood Catiline, who had willed the safety of the Capitol, the
temples and the whole city and people of Rome' (*Against
Catiline* III, 21). The same idea can be found in a speech
which Livy attributes to Camillus nearly 400 years
earlier. In this speech Camillus is made to dissuade the
Romans from emigrating after the disastrous sack of
Rome by the Gauls in 386 B.C. 'Can the Feast of Jupiter
be performed elsewhere than on the Capitol? . . . One
thing is certain: the good fortune of this site cannot be
transferred to any other place' (V, 52–4). The reasons
which Livy gives will have meant something special to
his readers, because there were repeated rumours from
the time of Julius Caesar onwards of proposals to build a
new capital city in the East. Rome's destiny and function
were impersonated in Jupiter Optimus Maximus, who
had taken up residence in the Capitoline temple. It was
for this reason that every year the new consuls, on entering office, went in procession to perform a sacrifice to
him and that every year the first meeting of the Senate
was held in his temple. Nothing illustrates his special
role better than the story told by Aulus Gellius (VI, 1,
6) about Scipio Africanus. Scipio used to have the shrine
of Jupiter unlocked for him before dawn and he would
go in and commune alone with the god about matters of
state. The guard-dogs, which barked at other visitors,
always treated him with respect.

The strength of this kind of feeling can be gauged by
the emotions of people who were forced to leave their
home-towns and, as they thought, the protection of the
patron god resident there. There is a moving scene in
Livy (I, 29), as the population of Alba Longa is evicted
(about 700 B.C.). The climax of their distress is reached
when they pass the temples and 'leave their gods behind
as it were prisoners'. There is the same intensity in

Ovid's complaint from exile in Tomi in A.D. 8–12 as he says 'good-bye for ever to the temples that my eyes shall never see again and to the gods of great Rome that I must leave behind' (*Tristia* I, 3, 33ff.).

Roman religion was concerned with success not with sin. 'Jupiter is called Best and Greatest,' Cicero comments (*On the nature of the gods* III, 87), 'because he does not make us just or sober or wise but healthy and rich and prosperous.' Happiness was the aim of life and happiness depended upon the successful outcome of all one's day-to-day activities, in private life, in business or agriculture and in the wider sphere of national affairs, and not upon one's moral condition. Since these activities could not be scientifically controlled and thus guaranteed to succeed, they were attributed to divine supervision, and the object of religion was to discover the correct procedure for securing the goodwill of the gods in making these activities successful. In this it has much in common with Christianity before it was modified by scientific discovery and by Protestantism, with its preoccupation with individual conscience and salvation. There is still, as H. J. Rose pointed out, a surviving tradition of the old religion in Catholicism: 'St. Agatha is popularly invoked to cure pains in the uterus, St. Apollonia to cure toothache, St. Clare can help sore eyes, St. Eutropius dropsy, St. Helena haemorrhage' (*Ancient Roman Religion*, p. 152). The Roman religious spirit is perfectly evoked by Horace (*Odes* I, 9): 'Let us make ourselves as comfortable as we can,' he goes on:

> Leave everything else to the gods. The moment
> they still the winds brawling
> on the boiling sea, the cypresses stop waving
> and the old ash trees.[1]

The gods are concerned with the powerful forces of nature. Man cannot hope to understand or control these forces. All that he can do is to hope for the best and to win the co-operation of the gods. It is this state of mind which Lucretius wants to change, as he sees men so

[1] Translated by David West: *Reading Horace*.

impressed by the starry heaven or natural disasters or even their own sense of helplessness in the face of the infinite that they grovel on the ground before the gods as the cause of these events (*On the nature of things* VI, 52*ff*.).

There was another very good reason why the Romans did not look to their gods to make them morally better. Their psychology was based on the assumption that a man's character is something fixed, something given to him at birth. Nothing could ever fundamentally alter that character or the actions which flowed from it. At best a man might be shamed or coerced into acting contrary to his true bent (*suum ingenium*) but it would never constitute a radical change of heart. It is only this that can explain the apparent irrelevancies, for instance, of Cicero's speeches. He tells us about Caelius' good behaviour on other occasions (which has no bearing on the charge under discussion) in order to convince the jury that it would have been 'out of character' (and so impossible) for Caelius to have done what he was accused of. Similarly Tacitus could not envisage that Tiberius' character might have deteriorated: if he ended as a tyrant, he must have been a tyrant all along (*Annals* VI, 51, 6) and any appearances to the contrary were mere pretence. Against such a background there was no point in asking the gods to make a man better. He was what he was because he was born that way. Religion might make a man more humble, by showing up human weakness in comparison with the great powers of nature, but it would not convert him to a new way of life. There is no reason to disbelieve Horace when he attributed his return to religion to the sudden sense of the overwhelming might of god. The occasion was a freak thunderstorm (*Odes* I, 34). Before that he had been 'a sparing and occasional worshipper' (*parcus deorum cultor et infrequens*). He does *not* say that it made him more virtuous.

So too, because matters of right and wrong were much less important in the struggle to achieve happiness than mastery of the forces around you, there is practically no evidence from the Augustan period or earlier to suggest that your chances of conciliating the gods depended upon your moral character. There were prescribed methods of treating with the gods which had been proved efficacious by experience, but, provided that you followed them scrupulously, it did not matter whether you were yourself good or bad or whether your prayers were for worthy ends. Prayers will be heard if they are correctly formulated rather than if they come from a penitent and unselfish heart. It was not until the following century when traditional religion had been more thoroughly coloured by philosophy and by oriental beliefs that Persius could assert that the only acceptable offering to the gods was 'holiness of mind and purity of heart' (*Satires* II, 73–4) or the younger Pliny could write: 'The gods rejoice more in the innocence of worshippers than in elaborate prayers; the man who enters their temples with a pure heart is more agreeable to them than one who recites a carefully prepared litany' (*Panegyric* 3). Such sentiments sound respectable but they are irrelevant to the central idea of Roman religion, and it is worth remembering that, according to Christian belief also, God's grace has never been confined to the good.

The simple belief that divine forces were operating all the time in every activity of the individual and the group was refined by Stoicism, the most influential philosophical movement at Rome in the first century B.C. Stoic thinkers, above all perhaps Posidonius (who died *c.* 50 B.C.) who taught Cicero, worked out a theological framework which made sense of the thousands of separate actions. There was a single rational spirit, a 'world-soul', which pervaded everything and of which the human mind-soul was a part. God penetrated the nature of everything (Cicero, *On the nature of the gods* II, 70–2) or, as Virgil expressed it (*Georgics* IV, 221*ff.*):

> God passes through all lands, all tracts of sea and the depths of the sky.

In this way all activity, and in particular all human activity, partook of the divine. It was merely a convention to label agricultural processes as 'Ceres', marine phenomena 'Neptune', distinguishing individual gods in this way. Moreover, since man himself contained part of this divine spirit, he could devise right relationships with 'god': for, in a sense, he was born from 'god'.

This noble and appealing philosophy, with its insistence on the rationality of the natural order which anticipates the way in which modern scientific laws have restricted the irrational intervention of God, made traditional religion intellectually respectable. The same set of religious formulae and procedures could be accepted as valid by a naive and illiterate slave and by a highly sophisticated man of education. They might justify them in different ways but they accepted them because, in the last resort, they worked. A logical consequence was that almost everything that anybody did was—in theory at least—a religious act which had to be attended by the proper religious ceremonies. To drive a nail into a piece of wood required not only a good nail, a good hammer and good co-ordination of hand and eye but also a well-tried ritual: otherwise the nail might bend or the deity concerned see to it that you hit your thumb. Furthermore—again, in theory at least—this applied equally to private actions performed by individuals or small groups and to public actions involving the state collectively. Cicero says that no important thing was undertaken even of a domestic kind without securing the assent of the gods (*On divination* I, 28) and Valerius Maximus, writing under the emperor Tiberius, makes the same assertion (II, 1, 1): 'Our forefathers did nothing either in public or private without first ascertaining the will of heaven.' This is no doubt pious exaggeration.

In practice, of course, people will have varied greatly in the conscientiousness of their family devotions, and, except in times of great national anxiety or rejoicing, it was not easy for the ordinary citizen to feel personally involved in the public worship offered on behalf of the state, particularly since many of the rituals were no longer related to his day-to-day needs. The townsman wanted as much as anyone a regular supply of cheap bread but, since he was not responsible for growing it

and probably, like his modern counterpart, had only
seen a farm on occasional visits to the country, it was
difficult for him to get worked up about public festivals
intended to eliminate blight. Horace does, indeed, give
us a glimpse of himself at a loose end in the Forum one
day 'dropping in on a service' (*Satires* I, 114), but it was
boredom, not interest, that drove him to it, and the girls
who hung around the temples of Rome did so not out of
piety but in the hope of picking up 'dates' (Propertius
II, 19, 10). What the Romans did—as far as public
activities were concerned—was to delegate the responsibility for ensuring that divine approval was won to
official authorities. It was left to the magistrates and
priests to see that all the rituals were conducted and the
ordinary citizen had no obligation at all to attend to
them or to take any interest in them. The only religious
duty enforced on everyone was not onerous: to avoid
work and to keep the peace on days of religious significance (holidays). This might have led to religion becom-
ing so remote from the life of the community that it
faded from view, tended only by a priestly class, but
Rome was unusual in allowing almost all its priesthoods
to be held by men actively engaged in public affairs and
in putting the chief responsibility for taking decisions
about religious issues not upon the priests as such but
upon the magistrates. It was as consul, not as *pontifex
maximus*, that Caesar offered sacrifice to Jupiter Optimus Maximus on 1 January 44 B.C. So there was never at
Rome any division between a priestly class and a govern-
ing class: indeed by the first century B.C., as we can judge
from Cicero's pleasure on being elected an augur, the
great priesthoods were regarded as social distinctions
more than religious offices, although they entailed
religious duties and required religious knowledge. The
Prime Minister could simultaneously be Archbishop of
Canterbury—and often was.

Public religion, therefore, could be looked after without the public being involved. It became part of the
standard routine of the magistrates or appropriate
officials to perform whatever public act of worship was

prescribed. Before entering on office or setting out on a campaign, before holding a census or an important assembly, the appropriate magistrate, as part of his recognised duty, took steps—on behalf of the state—to conciliate the gods. This is illustrated by a revealing story. When Pompey became consul in 70 B.C. he was comparatively inexperienced in civilian affairs. His career had been a military one—violent and successful. In order to prepare himself for his office, he commissioned Varro to write a small handbook telling him what to do (Aulus Gellius XIV, 7, 9). The book does not survive but we know that in it Varro stressed the importance of regular prayers as an introduction to public meetings and advised him always to ensure that religious matters were the first item on the Senate's agenda. A further indication of the weight which Romans attached to the proper performance of religious duties in state affairs is given by Cicero's reaction to the behaviour of Crassus. Crassus had been appointed governor of Syria as part of a deal with Pompey in 54 B.C. but his appointment aroused vocal opposition at Rome. To escape this, he tried to leave Rome unobtrusively, without having gone through the usual ceremonies, but his departure was detected by a tribune, Ateius Capito, who solemnly invoked curses on him. Crassus disregarded the implications of this inauspicious start and carried on with his journey. It was not surprising, Cicero concludes, that he came to grief at Carrhae (*On divination* I, 24).

In all affairs success depended upon divine co-operation and it was the object of religion to bring about that co-operation. There were three main means, common both to private and public religion, which were employed to regulate the relationship between men and gods: prayer, by which a request could be brought to the notice of the gods; sacrifice, by which the gods could be induced to yield a request and could be strengthened to execute it; and divination (in all its forms), by which the will of the gods could be known by men. All these were intricate procedures, evolved by centuries of faith and experience, which together formed the body of religious practice or *ius divinum*, as it was known. They were carefully compiled by a college of priests (the *pontifices*) and jealously handed down from generation to generation, because on them the prosperity of the whole community depended. The first step in founding a new city was to fix its religious calendar and to determine its festivals and priesthoods. Provision for this was, for example, expressly made by Caesar when creating a colony at Urso in Spain (*C.I.L.* II, 5439). By following the procedures of the *ius divinum* it was believed that the right relationship with the gods could be maintained. The Romans called this equilibrium or right relationship 'the peace of the gods'—*pax deorum*—and in a sensitive speech in the mouth of Ap. Claudius (the dramatic date is 368 B.C.) Livy gives fine expression to the ideals behind it: 'People nowadays may ridicule religious ceremonies, "What does it matter," they say, "if the sacred chickens don't eat or are slow in leaving their coop." These are trivial things. But our ancestors made Rome great by not despising these trivial things, whereas we profane all rituals, as if there was no longer any need for the peace of the gods' (VI, 41). Two hundred years later a consul, Q. Marcius Philippus, is made to say, 'The gods look kindly on the scrupulous observance of religious rites which have brought our country to its peak' (XLIV, 1, 11). The thought is a truly religious one because it emphasises man's dependence in everything that he does on God.

2

Prayer

GODS, like dogs, will only answer to their names. Living as we do in an age in which numbers (national health numbers, bank account numbers, telephone numbers etc.) identify people more easily than names, it is hard for us to understand the power which more primitive people attribute to names. But a trivial example of the survival of this idea is given by Ronald Knox when he points out how boys at school often try to conceal their Christian names and prefer to be called by a nick-name, because to reveal your Christian name is to give other boys a hold over you.[1] The same idea lies behind the Gnat's advice to Alice to lose her name: 'For instance, if the governess wanted to call you to your lessons, she would call out "Come here——", and there she would have to leave off, because there wouldn't be any name for her to call, and of course you wouldn't have to go, you know.'

The invocation of a god by name has always been the central feature of prayer and magic. If you know the name of the god, you can make him listen. It survives in Christianity. In the Old Testament the name of Jehovah was for long a secret name, not to be named or written, because it was too powerful. In the New Testament the superstition is eliminated but believers 'who call upon the name of the Lord' will be saved. We still pray 'in the name of the Father, and of the Son, and of the Holy Ghost'. In Roman (and Greek) religion, the first task was to discover the name of the god whom the worshipper wished to influence and to invoke that name. As Augustine, quoting Varro, who wrote 400 years earlier, puts it: 'We will be able to know what god we should invoke in every circumstance so that we don't

[1] *Pastoral Sermons*, p. 37.

behave like comedians who pray for water from Bacchus and for wine from the Nymphs' (*City of God* IV, 22). Given the complicated nature of Roman belief, by which almost every activity was thought to be divinely controlled, it needed considerable ingenuity to be able to choose the appropriate deity when required. It was for this reason that the *pontifices* compiled the elaborate and largely artificial lists of *Indigitamenta* as an exhaustive handbook of invocations for use on every occasion. But even this did not necessarily resolve doubts. In the second Ode of the first book, quoted earlier, Horace expresses uncertainty as to which god is the right god to summon to restore the tottering fortunes of Rome (cf. lines 25–6, *quem vocet divum populus ruentis/ imperi rebus*). Should it be Apollo, Venus, Mars or Mercury?

Some gods were so powerful that their names were never spoken, because of the harm that they might do to the community if they were successfully invoked. Such spirits were *nefandi,* unmentionable. It is this kind of fear that lies behind the proverb 'Talk of the Devil and he will appear'. Daemons of the underworld were sometimes known as 'The Great Name' or 'the Holy Name that is not uttered'. Other gods are too precious to the state or to the group for their names to be publicly divulged in case they should be summoned by one's enemies. Normally Jupiter Optimus Maximus was the patron god of Rome, but the city itself was also thought of as a deity, a deity, however, so valuable that it had a secret name, known only to the *pontifices*, for which 'Rome' was a cover-name. We do not know what that secret name was. As Servius says, 'The Romans wanted to conceal the identity of the god who looked after Rome and therefore their priestly discipline laid down that the gods of Rome should not be invoked by their proper names, for fear they should be enticed away.'

But most gods were approachable. The difficulty was to ensure that the god who was approached was invoked by the right name. Apollo might have changed his name or be using an alternative name, in which case he would not answer to a simple 'Apollo'. The Romans employed two techniques to safeguard themselves against this danger. The first was to list, as fully as possible, all the known alternatives which a god might use. In Poem 34 Catullus invokes the aid of Diana, but to be certain of securing her attention he goes on:

> You are called Juno Lucina
> by women in childbirth,
> you are called nightly Trivia, and Luna
> whose light is not your own.[1]

In more formal terms, this would be 'Diana, Latonia, Juno Lucina, Trivia, Luna'.

The second technique to prevent the god from evading a summons was to add at the end of the invocation a blanket-expression such as 'or whatever name you care to be called'. Catullus ends his list of Diana's names with the words 'by whatever name you please, be hallowed' (*Sis quocunque tibi placet sancta nomine*; 34, 21–2), in the same way that a pontifical formula, quoted by Servius (*On the Aeneid* II, 351), invokes 'Jupiter Optimus Maximus or by whatever other style you wish to be addressed' (*sive quo alio nomine te appellari volueris*). There are many inscriptional examples of this usage. A lead tablet, found near Arezzo, contains a horrific curse called down upon a certain Q. Letinius Lupus: the powers which are invoked to execute the curse are 'Hot Waters or Nymphs or by what other name you wish to be called' (*sive quo alio nomine voltis appellari*). The formulation is exactly in line with that used by the *pontifices*. The theology behind it finds one of its most noble expressions in a Chorus of Aeschylus' *Agamemnon*:

> Zeus, whoever He is, if this
> Be a name acceptable,
> By this name I will call him.
>
> (lines 160–2)

---

[1] Translated by David West.

When there was a strong suspicion that a place or an activity was in the charge of a god but it did not prove possible to establish the identity of the god for certain, the Romans resorted to the honest expedient of recognising an 'unknown god'. St. Paul mocked the Athenians for this superstition: 'For as I passed along and observed the object of your worship, I found also an altar with this inscription, TO AN UNKNOWN GOD. What therefore ye worship in ignorance, this set I forth unto you' (*Acts* XVII, 23). But it was a conscientious superstition, one that recognised the hand of a god at every crisis of the world. Evander, quoted above (p. 13), sensed that the woods of Rome were inhabited by a god but was uncertain what god it was. So Aulus Gellius tells us that in the event of an earthquake the Romans held a festival of purification without naming the god in whose honour it was given, for fear that they might make matters worse by naming the wrong god (II, 28, 2). They addressed simply 'the responsible deity', as a letter might be addressed 'to whom it may concern'. When Valerius engaged a giant Gaul in single combat, he received unexpected assistance in the form of a raven which settled on the Gaul's helmet and put him off his stroke. Valerius recognised it as divine intervention and prayed that 'whatever deity had sent the bird, whether it be a god or a goddess, should be gracious to him' (Livy VII, 26, 4). Such uncertainty must often have faced Romans when they travelled abroad and visited unfamiliar countries. A tribune called Julius Victor, stationed at Risingham in Northumberland, cautiously set up a dedication to 'the gods who inhabit this place' (*R.I.B.* 1208).

But there was no guarantee that this unknown deity would be male. If a goddess in fact resided there, she might not merely ignore a prayer couched in the masculine gender but be positively insulted by the mistake. To avoid such a danger the Romans refined the idea of 'the unknown god' still further by a stereotyped formula 'if it be a god or a goddess who (lives here)' (*si deus si dea*), which is found, for example, in an ancient prayer recommended by the elder Cato when a clearing

had to be made in a wood ('whether thou art a god or a
goddess, since this is a sacred grove, I make a peace-
offering to thee') or in the great prayer that was used to
persuade the guardian deity of Carthage to abandon the
city and so to break the power of Carthage once and for
all ('whether it is a god or a goddess in whose care are
the people and state of Carthage').

As a final precaution, especially on momentous occasions of state, it was usual to invoke all the other gods
collectively, after naming the special gods in whose province the matter was likely to lie. Although it was
normally expected the gods would limit themselves to
particular functions, there was no compelling reason
why they should do so and they are often found extending their sphere of activity. It was, therefore, as well to
be on the safe side, leaving nothing to chance. A further
reason may have been a sense that the gods formed a
collective group and, if so disposed, could help each
other in their operations. So the *pontifices* had a rule
always to invoke all the gods as a whole after individual
invocations (Servius, *On the Georgics* I, 21). Traces of
this custom can be seen in some of the prayers which
survive, for instance, in the comprehensive, if modern-
ised, formula used when war was declared (Livy I, 32,
10): 'Hearken, Jupiter, and you, Janus Quirinus, and
all the gods of heaven, of earth and of the underworld:
I call you to witness that such-and-such a people is in
the wrong.' Even Cicero, at the opening of a difficult
case, prays for indulgence from Jupiter Optimus Maximus 'and all the other gods and goddesses' (*For Rabirius
charged with treason* 5). Such formulae find a literary
echo in the great Ode which Horace composed for the
Secular Games of 17 B.C. In the concluding stanza he pro-
claims his confidence that 'Jupiter *and all the gods* have
heard' their prayers (lines 73–4).

The same god might have different functions. Janus
both opened and closed doors and it would be useless to
invoke Janus Patulcius if you were anxious to keep the
horses in the stable. The problem was accentuated in
the case of a god of many parts like Apollo or Jupiter.

Great care had to be taken to invoke not merely Apollo but Apollo with the requisite functional cult-title. Otherwise he might not listen. Macrobius, a pagan scholar of the middle fifth century A.D. who preserves much valuable learning of older times, explains that the successful combination of titles used by the Vestal Virgins for invoking Apollo to cure disease was 'Apollo Medice, Apollo Paean' (Apollo Doctor, Apollo Healer). No other combination, presumably, would work.

The greater gods had their favourite haunts, many of which were overseas as a result of the identification of Greek and Roman gods and the resulting attachment of Greek myths to the old, native beliefs. Apollo had at least one home in Rome and Augustus built him another splendid temple on the Palatine Hill, but his main residences were at Delphi and on the Aegean island of Delos. In directing their prayers the Romans were careful, if they could, to put the right address on them, or, at least, a series of alternative addresses in the hope of catching the god at home. It would be useless to invoke Poseidon in his golden home at Aegae if, as in the opening of Homer's *Odyssey*, he had left for a visit to the Ethiopians. The prayer would be returned to the sender, unopened. So after the invocation of the god's name, his residence or residences were given, usually in a relative clause. When Horace (*Odes* IV, 6, 26) calls on Apollo, as god of Music, to defend him, he phrases his prayer: 'Lyre-playing Phoebus, teacher of clear-voiced Thalia, you who wash your hair in the river Xanthus' (i.e. who inhabit Lycia whose principal river is the Xanthus). Similarly Virgil addresses a prayer to 'Mother Vesta, who watch over the Etruscan Tiber and the halls of Rome', and Lucretius begins his work with a prayer to 'Venus, who inhabit beneath the gliding stars the ship-bearing sea and the fruitful lands'.

The first task was to secure the ear of the god. The next was to convince the god that the request was a reasonable one and within his competence to fulfil. Genuine prayer never degenerates into magic by which a spell or formula, if correctly delivered, will of itself automatically manipulate the forces of nature. Prayer does not presume a favourable result; it recognises that divine goodwill is the first requirement and that this goodwill will not always or necessarily be forthcoming. In prayer the suppliant humbly beseeches a god for favours which may—for good reason—be refused; he does not demand them. In such petitions success would no doubt depend to a large extent on the acceptability of what the human had to offer in return, but it was a good argument, wherever possible, to advance reasons why a god should consider a request sympathetically. The two most effective reasons were: (a) he had granted it in the past, (b) it was clearly in his competence to grant it on this occasion. Catullus' prayer to Diana, which has been used before as an illustration, concludes with a typical example of (a):

> *as in the past,*
> protect by your gracious help
> the race of Romulus

When the Romans woke one morning in 460 B.C. to find that the Capitol had been seized by a band of slaves and Sabine mercenaries, the consul, P. Valerius, was faced with the job of restoring public morale. He did so by an appeal to Romulus 'to give the same determination to your descendants that you showed yourself when the Sabines once forced their way into the Capitol by bribery'. If there was no relevant precedent, a more general appeal to (b) might be tried. Aeneas asks the Sibyl to have pity on him and on his father and prays to be allowed to visit his father among the dead: for, he says to the Sibyl, 'you have all power'. Propertius prays to Bacchus to help him drown his sorrows, for 'you can subdue the arrogance of the wild goddess Love' (III, 17, 3) in just the same way that when Tibullus asks Isis to help him he appeals to the great quantity of pictures in her temples which prove that she can help her devotees when she is inclined to (I, 3, 27).

Then follows the request itself. Obviously it might

take many forms, depending upon the needs and the circumstances of the applicant. It might be for some specific
object or it might be for more general favour. The essential nature of a Roman prayer is perhaps best grasped
by reading a few of the surviving examples. The elder
Cato, in his handbook on agriculture, includes several
prayers for use in the daily management of the farm.
One of the most elaborate is a prayer addressed to Mars,
a god concerned as much with protecting the fields as
with winning battles, whom the farmer wishes to purify
his fields:

> Father Mars, I pray and beseech thee that thou mayest
> be propitious and well-disposed to me, our home and
> household, for which cause I have ordered the offering of
> pig, sheep and ox to be led round my field, my land and
> my farm, that thou might prevent, ward off and avert
> diseases, visible and invisible, barrenness and waste, acci-
> dent and bad water, that thou wouldest permit the crop
> and fruit of the earth, the vines and shrubs to wax great
> and prosper, that thou wouldest preserve the shepherds
> and their flocks in safety and give prosperity and health
> to me and our house and household; for all these causes
> . . . be increased by the sacrifice of this offering of sucking
> pig, lamb and calf. (Cato, *On agriculture* 142: adapted
> from Cyril Bailey's translation.)

This is a prayer for 'blessing on the farm', of a kind that
must have been standard in the country at most periods
of Roman paganism: in its fundamentals it is very
similar to a prayer which Ovid expressed in verse in
connexion with the festival of the Parilia (*Fasti* IV, 735–
82). But Augustan Rome was an urban and an imperial
society, whose concerns were no longer with the simple
business of the farm but with more public prosperity.
There is a prayer which Augustus offered in 17 B.C. on
the occasion of the Secular Games:

> O Fates . . . I beseech and pray you, just as you have
> increased the Empire and the majesty of the Roman
> people, the Quirites, in war and peace, so may the Latins

ever be obedient; grant everlasting safety, victory and
health to the Roman people, the Quirites; protect the
Roman people, the Quirites, and keep safe and sound the
state of the Roman people, the Quirites; be favourable
and propitious to the Roman people, the Quirites, the
Board of Fifteen, to me, to my house and my household;
and deign to accept this sacrifice of nine ewes and nine
female goats, perfect for sacrificing. For all these causes
be increased by the sacrifice . . .

Despite the changed conditions, the basic form of it is
similar to Cato's. Many of the same phrases recur ('me,
my house and my household', 'give prosperity and
health', 'for all these causes be increased' etc.) and the
same pattern is followed throughout. Personal prayers—
for obvious reasons—are less often recorded, but there is
a heart-felt plea from someone in Spain who had had his
clothes stolen:

Goddess Proserpine Ataecina who inhabit the town of
Turobriga, I beg, pray and beseech you by your majesty
to revenge the theft that has been committed against me
and to [punish with a terrible death] whoever has borrowed, stolen or made away with the articles listed below:
six tunics, two cloaks . . .

The standard elements are clearly seen in this prayer
—the careful naming and location of the goddess, and the
reminder ('by your majesty') that it is in the goddess'
power to perform the request. Private prayers are usually
simple, like that uttered by a certain L. Aufidius to
Hercules, 'You are a holy god; help him who asks you
for your peace,' or one, cited by the Christian apologist
Arnobius as typical of pagan prayers, 'Draw near, draw
near, Penates and you, Apollo, and you, Neptune, and
by the mercy of your godhead avert all these evils by
which I am consumed, tortured and vexed.'

In addition to requests for positive favours, two other
types of prayer are worth noticing. The first does not so
much ask for the grant of a good as for the avoidance of
an evil. It is entirely negative in outlook. Most of us
would be content if instead of receiving occasional

'windfalls' from heaven we managed to escape the un-
called-for accidents and disasters which are apt to occur,
often for no good reason, at work or in the family or
even as a consequence of some national upheaval. It
would be much more appropriate that these things
should happen to our enemies, to those who wish us ill.
The Romans felt this acutely and designed (on Greek
models) a special form of prayer to achieve it. The god
is asked to deflect the evil and send it on to someone else.
Catullus ends his terrifying account of what happened
to Attis when he was inspired by Cybele, with the
prayer: 'May your frenzy never come near my house,
goddess; excite others, make others mad.' The theme is
common in Horace who begs Apollo and Diana to
divert war, pestilence and famine from the Roman
people on to Persia and Britain (*Odes* I, 21, 13–16), or
who prays that the wives and children of Rome's enemies
may feel the effect of natural disasters sent by the gods
(*Odes* III, 27, 21–4), or who, in a humorous mood,
earnestly prays Venus to leave him alone in favour of
younger and more suitable devotees (*Odes* IV, 1, 1–8).
The spirit of such prayers is well caught by Livy when
he makes the Romans, in a moment of panic after an
unexpected reverse, 'ask the gods to ward off destruction
from the homes, the temples, and the walls of Rome and
to direct the peril instead upon Veii' (V, 18, 12).

On the whole, however, the Augustan age was not
vindictive. Their prayers were civilised, seeking neither
excessive favours for themselves nor malicious misfor-
tunes for their enemies but rather asking humbly that
they might continue to enjoy what they had, unmolested
and in peace. On his return to Rome after the resound-
ing victory of Actium, Augustus was welcomed with a
great show of solidarity by the Senate. His reply was
characteristic: 'I have achieved all my hopes; what else
am I to pray the immortal gods to give me than that I
should be permitted to enjoy their unanimous support
until the very end of my life' (Suetonius, *Augustus* V, 8,
2). Similarly the ritual prayer which was spoken every
five years, when the census was taken, asked that the gods

should preserve the prosperity of Rome intact for ever (Valerius Maximus IV, 1, 10). This formulation, it was said, had been imposed by the great Scipio Africanus in place of an earlier one that prayed for 'a further extension of Roman prosperity'. Rome, Scipio said, was fine and large enough already.

To enjoy what he has in good health, that is Horace's heart-felt prayer to Apollo (*Odes* I, 31, 17), which he repeats in a later *Satire* with the moving comment, 'I ask no more' (*nil amplius oro*; *Satires* II, 6, 4). For behind every success and every good fortune there lurked in the Roman mind a fear of provoking the jealousy of the gods. The premature death of Marcellus, Augustus' favourite nephew, in 23 B.C. caused widespread and genuine grief and prompted Virgil to reflect that the gods must have been jealous, 'for Rome would have seemed too powerful in their eyes if such gifts had been hers for ever' (*Aeneid* VI, 870–1). It was this fear that prompted the luckless Camillus, when at last he had taken Veii, to pray that 'any god who felt that his success and the success of the Roman people was too great, would abate his jealousy and not satisfy it at the expense of Rome' (Livy V, 21, 15). It survived right down to the end of the pagan world. A little handbook of Roman history, compiled by a certain Festus in the late fourth century, comments on the death of the emperor Carus: 'His victory over the Persians seemed too mighty for the powers above. It was thought to have aroused divine jealousy and wrath. In the full flush of victory he was struck dead by lightning' (*A Breviary of Roman History* 24). When the gods *are* jealous, their vengeance is greedy (Horace, *Odes* I, 2, 37 (Mars), *heu nimis longo satiate ludo*).

The contents of prayers, then, are, as we would expect, of many kinds but they all have in common the same meticulous formulation. Just as every care had to be taken to ensure that the right god was correctly invoked, so the prayer itself had to be worded to cover every possibility. The Spaniard's clothes might not have been actually stolen: they might have been borrowed, in which case a request to punish the thief would be inapplicable. Cato's farmer specified exhaustively all the disasters that might strike his crops and his flocks, for fear that one should be overlooked and so not prevented; Augustus prayed for the 'everlasting safety, victory and health' of the Roman people. Roman prayers were phrased like legal documents, with repetitions, accumulated synonyms and detailed particularisations ('the Roman people, the Quirites'; 'me, my house and my household') to make sure that no loop-hole should be left. And when they were uttered the exact words had to be used; otherwise they would be invalid. A single slip (e.g. 'my house and me' instead of 'me, my house') or a single omission would be enough to wreck the whole exercise. In that event the only thing to do was to start all over again, perhaps with an additional prayer asking for forgiveness for having made the mistake. Livy records (XL, 16, 2) that because a magistrate from the Latin town of Lanuvium accidentally omitted the words 'the Roman people, the Quirites' in one of the sacrifices at the great festival of all the Latins, in 176 B.C., the whole festival had to be repeated—at the expense of Lanuvium—and Cicero hoped to persuade his audience that the attempt by his enemies to consecrate his house (and so deprive him of it for ever) was null and void because the youth who performed the ritual stammered (*On his house* 139). This concern for absolute accuracy was not confined to the Latins. We have nine bronze sheets, dating from about 200 B.C. to 80 B.C., from the Umbrian town of Iguvium (Gubbio) on which were inscribed the detailed instructions for rituals to be held there. The prayers are worded as precisely as Latin prayers and the same provision is laid down that if a mistake is made the priests had to go back to the beginning and start again.

Sometimes, when it was the duty of a magistrate or other 'lay' person who might not be practised at it to offer a complicated prayer, a professional priest was called on to lead off and the magistrate then repeated each sentence after him in a clear loud voice. This procedure (*praeire verba* 'to anticipate the words', as it was called) must have forestalled many expensive mistakes. The final precaution, taken particularly on large public occasions when there was liable to be a good deal of extraneous noise which might distract the god's attention, was to employ a flute-player who played throughout the prayer in order to drown other sounds (Pliny, *Natural History* XXVIII, 11). Suetonius notes as a sign of Tiberius' silliness, along with his pestering scholars to answer such questions as 'what name Achilles took when he served among the women' and 'what song the Sirens sang', the fact that he had no flute-player when, in a great show of religious fervour on the day after Augustus' death, he offered public prayers (*Tiberius* 70). It was a frightful thing if the player stopped in the middle (Arnobius, *Against the pagans* IV, 31).

Behind all this ritualism lay a profound anxiety to establish communication with the gods, which recognised that the gods were not easy to approach but that human happiness depended upon their co-operation. The Romans would never have gone to such detailed trouble if they had not believed that the form of prayer which they had evolved worked and, in that they believed that it worked, it did work. But they did not rely simply on the natural benevolence of the gods to grant their prayers as an act of grace. In so far as it was possible for human beings to do anything which would merit divine gratitude, the Romans tried to earn the benevolence of the gods. Prayers often state a claim which the suppliant has on the god's goodwill, as, for instance, Mopsus prays to Apollo (Ovid, *Metamorphoses* VIII, 350), 'Phoebus, if I have worshipped you and still do worship you, grant my request' or as Nisus invokes the aid of Diana in *Aeneid* IX, 406*ff.*, by reminding her of the gifts which his father had laid on her altars and the additional dedications which he had himself made in her temple. The claim is usually not the *moral* worth of the suppliant but his devotion to the god, his *pietas*. Catullus asks the gods as a return for his *pietas* to free him of his infatuation for Lesbia (76, 26); Anchises asks Jupiter for a sign, 'if our *pietas* has earned us one'

(*Aeneid* II, 690). This is the sense in which 'piety' is used throughout this book: it has nothing to do with good moral conduct.

But the most common way of influencing the gods was by sacrifice. The purpose and the forms of sacrifice will be examined in the next chapter. For the present it is only important to notice that the Romans connected prayer and sacrifice in two quite different ways. The first was a straightforward request accompanied by a sacrifice or a promise of a sacrifice—'Please, hear my prayer: I am sacrificing (or I will sacrifice) a lamb etc. to you.' This is the form that is used, for example, in both Cato's and Augustus' prayer: 'Be favourable and propitious to me, to my house and my household . . . for all these causes be increased by the sacrifice of a sucking pig, lamb and calf.' And it is the form that was followed on all the ordinary family occasions when prayer and sacrifice were offered before meals or on festivals. The sacrifice is made as a free-will offering without any attempt to blackmail the god into acceding to the prayer. There is no suggestion of a threat, 'you had better listen to me because I am giving you these presents'. It is at once a dignified and a trusting relationship. A god, because he is a god, is entitled to the best that man can offer and a man can only do his duty and hope for divine favour. At its finest it is not significantly different from the Christian's relationship with his Maker.

The Romans, however, also had another approach to the god. They vowed or promised that, *if* a god performed a certain request, then they for their part would make an offering in return. The vow was a contractual relationship and the sacrifice ceased to be a free-will offering and became instead the fulfilment of a covenant. But it was not a degrading relationship which reduced the gods to puppets. In actual practice, as can be seen by studying the thousands of surviving inscriptions which record the performance of a vow, the predominant note still is one of humility and gratitude, and the gift or sacrifice that is paid is one that has been chosen in the sincere belief that it will please the god. A slave who prayed for his freedom 'vowed as a slave and paid as a free man' (*servos vovit liber solvit; C.I.L.* X, 1569): in four Latin words there is a wealth of religious feeling. Equally, it was not a relationship which reduced the suppliant to a menial status. There is a splendid self-confidence and dignity about the bargain which Propertius strikes with Bacchus (III, 17): 'If you cure me of love, I will sing your praises in my poetry throughout the world.'

In making a private vow, the Roman would write his request and the promised offering on a wax tablet which he would tie to the knee of a statue of the god concerned (Apuleius, *Apology* 54; Juvenal, *Satires* X, 55). At this stage he was said to be 'on trial for his vow' (*voti reus*). If the god did not answer the prayer, nothing more need be done and the whole business was forgotten; if the prayer was answered, then he paid his vow and set up a little memento of the happy outcome: he was then said to be 'condemned of his vow' (*voti damnatus*). Over and over again we meet inscriptions which contain simply the name of a god, the name of a person and the letters *v.s.l.m.* (*votum solvit libens merito*)—'so-and-so willingly paid his vow as was due to such-and-such a god'. Like the little thank-offering plaques set up to saints by his Catholic descendants, these dedications show the strength of the Roman's faith in the gods. And it pervades Latin literature, sometimes earnestly as when Cloanthus invokes the gods to help him in a boat-race (*Aeneid* V, 235–8): 'Gods who have dominion of the sea, over whose waters I speed, gladly will I set before your altars on this shore a white bull in payment of my vow and will cast the entrails on to the salt water [if I win]'); sometimes frivolously as when Horace protests that the votive tablet which, like a sailor saved from ship-wreck, he has dedicated on the temple wall shows that his stormy love-affair with Pyrrha is over (*Odes* I, 5, 13–16), or when Encolpius vows that he will give a pair of doves to Venus tomorrow 'if I can kiss this boy without his noticing' (Petronius, *Satires* 85).

Public vows tend to be more perfunctory and impersonal. Several of the vows which, under the Empire, were made for the emperor are preserved in the inscriptions recording the activities of the Arval Brethren (see p. 13). A typical one, made in A.D. 80, uses the formulae that had been standard for over a century:

> Jupiter Optimus Maximus, if the emperor Titus Caesar Vespasianus Augustus, *pontifex maximus,* holder of the tribunician power, father of his country, and Caesar Domitian, son of the deified Vespasian of whom we deem that we are speaking, should live and their house be safe on the next 1 January that comes to pass for the Roman people, the Quirites, and for the state of the Roman people, the Quirites, and you preserve that day and them safe from dangers (if there are or shall be any before that day) and if you have granted a felicitous issue in the manner that we deem that we are speaking of and you have preserved them in that present condition or better—and may you so do these things—then we vow that you shall have, in the name of the College of the Arval Brethren, two gilded oxen.

Only in times of crisis would such vows rise above the level of mechanical repetition, but crises did occur, not only in early days as when Ap. Claudius, consul in 296 B.C., in the middle of a desperate battle, raised his hands to heaven and cried, 'Bellona, if you grant us today the victory, I vow to dedicate a temple to you,' but also in the more sedate world of Horace and Virgil. The prayers for Augustus' safe return from the East in 19 B.C. were real enough: they were not merely demonstrations of loyalty to the régime.

The different aspects of prayer are perhaps best seen in the prayer with which Velleius Paterculus, a loyal officer under Tiberius, concluded his pocket *History of Rome*:

> Jupiter Capitolinus, and Mars Gradivus, the author and consolidator of the Roman name, and Vesta, guardian of the perpetual fires, and all the other gods who have raised this might of the Roman Empire to the furthest eminence

of the world, I pray and beseech you publicly: guard, preserve, protect this order, this peace, this prince and when he has fulfilled the full span of mortal life, ordain successors who in due time may be able to bear on their shoulders the burden of the Empire of the world with the steadfastness that we have seen him bear it. . . .

The appropriate gods are closely designated, their residence (Capitolinus) and functions defined; the other gods are invoked as well and a claim on their attention is established by reference to their past services. The prayer itself is couched in precise and exact language so that the gods cannot fail to know what is requested. But the spirit is humble, the request sincere.

I Sacrifice of a steer: from a stone relief in the Museo Archeo-
logico, Milan

II *Haruspex* examining entrails after sacrifice: from a stone relief in the Louvre

3
Sacrifice

IMAGINE 160,000 mooing, messy cows being led along Whitehall and then butchered in the forecourt of Westminster Abbey at a Coronation. Yet, according to Suetonius, Caligula's accession to the throne was celebrated by the sacrifice of that number of victims in three months on the Capitol. The idea revolts us, just as the thought of Horace being so grateful for a cool drink from the fountain of Bandusia that he vowed to sacrifice a young kid into its waters shocked A. Y. Campbell into exclaiming, 'Who wants a drink out of the fountain of Bandusia after that?' Sacrifice, especially blood-sacrifice, is so foreign to modern ways of thinking that it is impossible to recapture the faith of those like the ancient Jews or the Romans who believed it to be man's most effective means of influencing the gods.

Sacrifice means literally making something holy (*sacer*), setting it aside from all common usage and handing it over exclusively to the gods. A holy place is one reserved for a god where he has his residence: in the normal course of events men may not trespass there, just as there were no boats on Lake Vadimo because it was a holy lake (p. 14). In primitive times the ultimate sanction which the state could use against a criminal was to declare him 'holy', which meant that he was cut off from all human intercourse and could be killed with impunity in order that the gods might enjoy their property the sooner: effectively it was a death sentence. So, in worship, the believer chose out something special and gave it to the gods. But the basic difference between a sacrifice and a present of gold or jewellery was that what was given by way of sacrifice had to contain the principle of life. It need not be animal. Most of the offerings made to the gods in family cults were cereal—small

cakes (*strues*) made of spelt (*far*), a kind of wheat, or
flour mixed with salt (*mola salsa*). Horace mentions the
familiar domestic scene of 'the ritual spelt and the little
cake leaping in the flame' (*Odes* III, 23, 20) which Ovid
describes more fully as he tells how there was a break in
the main meal of the day when a small piece of food was
put on a plate and thrown into the fire to be consumed
by the household gods (*Fasti* VI, 307*ff*.). Other offerings
used in sacrifice included flowers, honey, cheese, fruit,
wine and milk. But animals were the most effective and
the most conspicuous.

The thought lying behind the choice of animate or
quasi-animate sacrifices was understandable. The gods
were essentially gods of activity—they did things, such as
controlling childbirth or repelling disease—and activity
requires vitality. If the gods' vitality was not sustained
and renewed, that activity would be weakened and they
would no longer be able to function efficiently. Crops
would fail or disease would spread because the relevant
gods did not have enough vigour to perform their tasks
even if they wanted to. Varro puts this quite simply
when he writes: 'I am afraid that some gods may perish
simply from neglect.' The existence of the gods depends
to an appreciable extent on man's devotion to them. In
the great prayers which were used when sacrifice was
offered such as Cato's and Augustus' quoted in the previous chapter, the key phrase is always 'be you increased'
(with this offering). The Latin word is *macte* which is
connected with *magnus* 'great' and similar words. The
worshipper is praying that his sacrifice may revitalise the
god and so enable him to fulfil the requests that are
made to him. Of all living things animals are the most
obviously vigorous and therefore the most potent sacrifices, and the most vital parts of an animal, the parts that
seem to contain the very spark of life, are the heart, liver,
kidneys etc. It was these that were usually offered to the
gods. It was a fortunate coincidence that, from a human
point of view, they are the least edible.

By the Augustan age, however, this underlying idea
had been supplanted by more mundane motives. It is

doubtful if Horace consciously wished to enhance the freshness of the fountain of Bandusia by sacrificing a kid. More probably he knew that a kid was the traditional sacrifice to a fountain-god (whatever the origin of the tradition may have been) and believed that because the goodwill of the gods had been secured in the past by doing things in the traditional way, one should go on doing them that way. Alternatively he may have thought of the gods as sharing his tastes and fancies and so have wanted to please them by giving them a share of the things which he enjoyed most.

At all events animal sacrifice was a regular feature of Roman life, and is constantly mentioned in the pages of writers like Virgil and Livy. It is, therefore, worth seeing exactly what happened. In the temples of Rome itself sacrifice was made by both magistrates and state officials in the regular round of public festivals and also by private individuals at their own expense, either in fulfilment of a vow, as Juvenal once sacrificed two white lambs to Juno Regina and Minerva and a young ox to Jupiter Capitolinus which he had vowed for the safe return of his friend Catullus, or, more rarely, as an accompaniment to a prayer. The procedure in each case was much the same. The choice of victim was, as Cicero tells us (*On the laws* II, 19), laid down in the manuals of the *pontifices* and depended partly upon the god involved and partly upon the reasons for the sacrifice. One invariable principle was that male animals were offered to gods and female to goddesses. Colour mattered as well: white for Juno and Jupiter, deities of the upper air, and black for the gods of the underworld; Lucretius speaks of men 'sacrificing black cattle and sending offerings to the gods below' and when Aeneas sacrifices to Anchises on the anniversary of his death he kills 'two black-backed oxen' (*Aeneid* V, 97). Size varied—sucking (*lactentes*) or grown (*maiores*)—according to the nature of the occasion. From the state festivals we can form an idea of the range of animals that were used—goats at the Lupercalia, two pregnant cows to Earth on 15 April, a red dog to Robigus on 25 April (the 'blight' god), a horse to Mars on 15 October, a bull, ram and boar at the conclusion of the census, and so on. The ordinary Roman could find out what was the appropriate animal for his vow by asking at the temple of the deity concerned. In each temple there seems to have been a list which set out the sacrifices that its deity would accept.

Faced with having to discharge a successful vow, he would begin by going to the temple to fix a convenient day with the custodian (*aedituus*), arrange for the professional officiators (the people who actually cut the throats and dissected the animals—*popae* and *victimarii*) to be in attendance, and hire a flute-player (*tibicen*). There were standard fees for their services. A law is still in existence that gives these details (*C.I.L.* VI, 820). Since most inhabitants of Rome did not possess country estates and could not have provided the requisite animals from their own resources, the next step was to go to the cattle market and buy a suitable beast. It had to be perfect: any deformity would be an insult to the god. On the great day, dressed in his toga, he would tie ribbons to its horns (or sometimes, if he was rich, gild them) and its tail and lead it through the streets to the temple. It was a good sign if it went willingly to the slaughter. Juvenal, for instance, speaks admiringly of his ox as tugging at its rope to get to the priest's knife. If, on the other hand, it struggled and tried to run away, it was evidently an inauspicious animal which would not find favour with the gods. He would have to sell it back, buy another and start again. Safely arrived at the temple, he would hand it over to the priests and the sacrifice proper would begin.

Ancient temples were in many ways the opposite of modern churches. In Roman Catholic churches the principal action, e.g. the Mass, takes place inside the sanctuary, but in temples the business was done outside. There were four main elements in a large temple. The centre of it was a walled room (*cella*) in which stood the statue of the god, often gaudily decorated with jewels and precious ornaments, the gifts of the faithful. Besides the statue there was nothing else except possibly

for a small altar on which incense could be burned.
There were no seats or other furniture. There were
often no windows and light was provided by a hole in
the ceiling. Some idea of the striking impression which
the statue, with its wealth of gold and silver glinting in
the dim light, must have made on a worshipper coming
in from the glare and the heat of the sun outside can
be derived from the experience of going into a Greek
Orthodox church today. Behind the *cella* there was a
room or rooms, which served like a sacristy or vestry
for the use of the attendants and for the safe-keeping of
treasures that were not on display in the *cella*. Even in
small temples these treasures might be very considerable. Hadrian found 3 lbs. of gold and 206 lbs. of silver
in a ruined temple at Lanuvium (*C.I.L.* XIV, 2088),
while the gifts which Augustus alone sent to five major
temples in Rome were valued at over 100,000,000
sesterces, perhaps £5,000,000 in equivalent modern
terms. In front of the *cella*, leading into it, was an ante-
room, usually open at the near end. This complex of
rooms was surrounded by a colonnade, normally oblong
in Italian temples, square in Romano-Celtic ones, which
served no functional purpose except to provide shelter
from the sun and the rain.

When a Roman made his vow, he entered the *cella*,
attached the wax tablets to the statue and then prayed
facing the statue and stretching out his arms to it, or in
moments of great emotion on his knees, like Tibullus
(I, 2, 85), or even grovelling on the floor in front of it as
Lucretius despises the superstitious for doing (V, 1200).
But where did he actually perform his sacrifice? Even in
the hands of expert practitioners this must have been a
bloody business. Curiously enough, the literary and the
archaeological evidence do not provide any clear answer.
It was not at the little altar in the *cella*. That is certain,
if only because it was too small and too much indoors.

We hear of a few 'sanctuary sacrifices' (Festus 356 L.)
but they were evidently exceptional. Normally, where
blood-sacrifices were offered, a stone altar was set up in
front of the temple, either at the foot of steps leading up

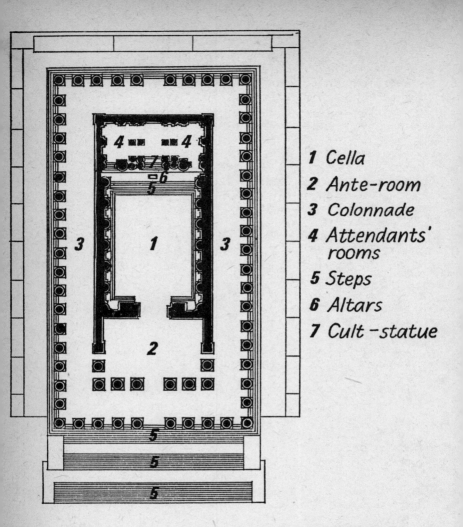

1 Cella

2 Ante-room

3 Colonnade

4 Attendants' rooms

5 Steps

6 Altars

7 Cult-statue

PLAN OF TEMPLE

6

to it or at the entrance to the ante-room. In primitive
times, a fresh altar was constructed from turfs for each
sacrifice and a memory of this survived into the Augustan age and beyond in the practice of putting a single
turf on top of the altar before a sacrifice. Roman temples
which had to cope with a constant succession of sacrifices
would have had large permanent altars made of stone.

The victim, then, was led before this altar on which a
good fire had been lit and the ritual began. The first
precaution was to ensure that no intruder was present
who might contaminate the proceedings. Women (and
dogs), for instance, were excluded from sacrifices to
Hercules and Mars (Plutarch, *Roman Questions* 60),
while slaves were only allowed to attend a small number of cults, such as that of Fortuna. It is unlikely that
all strangers were banned from being present, as one
ancient source (Servius, *On the Aeneid* VIII, 172) seems
to assert, but foreigners, i.e. non-Romans, may have
been, as being potentially dangerous enemies who
might cast an evil spell. This is laid down in the
Umbrian rites at Iguvium and explains the ritual cry
that all profane people should depart—*procul, o procul
este profani*, as the Sibyl cried when Aeneas performed
the sacrifice at the entrance to the Underworld. But the
worshipper would certainly have invited all his friends
to attend and join in the celebration. Next the priests
and those who are offering the sacrifice wash their hands
with holy water from a special stoup and dry them on
linen cloths. Great importance was attached to cleanli-
ness in sacrifice. Tibullus charged those coming to a
rural festival 'to come with clean clothes and to take
spring water in clean hands' (II, 1, 13–14) and Livy
(XLV, 5, 4) uses the language of Roman ritual when he
makes L. Atilius describe the religious observances of
Samothrace: 'Every sacrifice is introduced by the intima-
tion that those with unclean hands should depart.' This
detail explains the ruse employed to trick the Sabine
who came to sacrifice a wonderful cow to Diana in the
new temple which Servius Tullius had built (Livy I, 4,
5). The attendant indignantly told him to wash first and,

while he was away, seized his chance and sacrificed the cow himself.

Silence is now commanded (in state sacrifices a herald uttered an age-old cry *favete linguis*, 'check your tongues'), except for the steady music of the flute-player who is employed, as at times of solemn prayer, to drown extraneous noises. The priests cover their heads with the folds of their togas and take up a square wooden platter heaped with the sacred flour mixed with salt (*mola salsa*). They sprinkle the flour between the horns of the animal, as the attendants hold it, and on to the sacrificial knife. This action was called *immolare*. They might also—though this seems to have been optional— pour wine which was kept for the purpose, in a small moveable stand (*foculus*), over its head from a saucer (*patera*). Thus Dido, 'holding the saucer in her right hand, pours wine between the horns of a white cow' which she is sacrificing to Juno (*Aeneid* IV, 60–1). The animal is now stripped of its ribbons and decorations while an attendant symbolically draws a knife along its back from head to tail (Servius, *On the Aeneid* XII, 173). It was at this point in the service that the prayer seems to have been made—a prayer carefully written and rehearsed to avoid the danger of any mistake which might involve repetition of the whole ceremony. The suppliant, standing and turning to the right, delivered it in the direction of the cult-statue within the temple, just as Christians turn towards the altar when saying the creed. It was regarded as a sinister omen when Camillus slipped as he was turning to make a prayer after the capture of Veii (Livy V, 21, 16). The climax was now at hand. The *popa*, standing on the right of the animal, asked, 'Do I strike?' (*agone*) and, on receiving an affirmative answer, struck a well-aimed blow with a hammer at the animal's head which stunned it so that it sank on its knees to the ground. Then a knife-man (*cultrarius*), holding its head upwards if it was being offered to a heavenly god and downwards to a god of the Underworld, slit its throat. An ox has a lot of blood (about two gallons) and when its main artery is cut it spurts out.

We do not know how the Romans dealt with all the blood. It was evidently not well thought of if it did not run freely, for Virgil regards a sacrifice in which the blood barely stained the knife as an unmistakable failure (*Georgics* III, 492), and Lucretius (V, 1200) gives us a vividly gruesome picture of 'altars washed with the streaming blood of beasts', but the Romans can hardly have let it all gush onto the altar or else it would certainly have put the fire out. Some may have been caught in containers for later ritual use (so Aeneas' companions, when they sacrificed to Hecate, 'put knives to the animals' throats and catch the warm blood in vessels' (*Aeneid* VI, 248–9) and there are occasional references to the priest tasting the blood), some will have spurted on to the altar (the temple of Venus at Paphos in Cyprus was exceptional in that blood was not allowed to touch the altar; Tacitus, *Histories* II, 3), but most of it must have flowed to the ground and been washed away when all the proceedings were over.

The moment of death was a tense one and a clean kill was anxiously sought. A half-killed beast or a beast that ran away before it could be dispatched meant that the sacrifice was ruined. It required the insensitivity of a Julius Caesar to disregard the evil omen of a victim that ran away when he was sacrificing before a campaign against the African prince Juba (Suetonius, *Caesar* 59). When a similar thing happened to Vitellius as he was preparing to fight at Mevania, in A.D. 69, he took the hint and hurried home to Rome. If all had gone well so far, the animal was now dismembered and dissected. The internal organs were removed for careful examination to ensure that the inside was as perfect as the outside of the victim. Any fault would invalidate the ceremony, especially since these organs were the most vital parts of the animal, the parts which were earmarked for the god's consumption: it could also be an awful warning. When Caligula sacrificed on 1 January 41 A.D., part of the victim's liver was found to be missing: he was assassinated later that year. These organs, called *exta*, together sometimes with portions of the rest

of the carcase, were cut up into small pieces (*prosecta*)
and put on the altar for the gods to consume (*porricere*).
They were dissolved in flames. The problem now remained of disposing of the rest of the meat. If it was a
small animal, a goat or a lamb, it was not so difficult,
but an ox will feed up to a hundred people comfortably
and the Romans were not great meat-eaters. Tacitus
(*Annals* XIV, 24) comments on some troops who were
driven by hunger to eat meat, which suggests that it was
not a normal part of their diet, and this is confirmed
by the accounts of ordinary meals in Cicero or Juvenal.
In a very few cases the entire carcase was burnt on the
altar. This was called the 'Achaean rite' and is mentioned, for instance, in the detailed description of the
Secular Games of 17 B.C.

At most sacrifices the meat must have been eaten on
the spot by the priest and the man who offered the
sacrifice and his friends. We frequently hear of a kitchen
in the vicinity of a temple where it could have been
cooked, since the altar was too small, and also of a
dining-room (*cenaculum*) attached to the temple where
a meal could have been eaten. At state sacrifices, the
priest and the magistrates or even, if it was a great
occasion, the Senate and the whole people as well were
invited to the feast. But those 160,000 head of cattle
must have taken a lot of eating. It is also possible that,
except where it was specifically laid down that all the
meat had to be consumed on the premises as in sacrifices to Hercules and Silvanus, some of the meat found
its way back to the butchers and was sold to the ordinary
public. St. Paul devotes some time to the attitude of
the Corinthians when faced with eating sacrificial meat
from the market (I. *Corinthians* 8).

The procedure was detailed and exact, perfected by
centuries of tradition. In the hands of skilled priests a
sacrifice was probably both devout and moving. To
witness the moment of death, whether of a human being
or an animal, can be a highly emotional experience, as
the climax of a bull-fight shows. And the Romans
exercised every care to ensure that the whole ceremony

was dignified. A slip, a mistake, a blunder at any stage
entailed the repetition of the whole procedure (*instauratio*), together with an additional offering by way of
apology for the previous error (*piaculum*). Just as, if a
bit of the food thrown into the fire at an ordinary family
meal fell onto the floor, there was an 'atonement for
fallen food' (the bit had to be carefully picked up and
then returned to the flames), so Cato preserves a formula
for offering an atoning pig to Mars, if the original is
discovered to have some defect (*On agriculture* 141).
Livy records several occasions when the enormously
expensive Latin festival at which thirty Latin tribes
sacrificed on Mount Albano had to be repeated because
one of the tribes had been overlooked (e.g. XXXII 1, 9;
XXVII 3, 4). It was even possible to make a preliminary
sacrifice (*praecidanea*) to atone in anticipation for some
unintended slip. To appreciate the nightmarish things
that *could* go wrong, one has only to read the account of
Dido's sacrifice in the *Aeneid* (IV, 453ff.). The holy water
turned black, the wine turned to filthy blood, and so on.
The high standard of dignity was reinforced by the firm
belief that only accidental faults could be remedied. A
deliberate error was irremediable, as the learned lawyer
Scaevola stated. No atonement, Horace writes (*Odes* I,
28, 34), will absolve a man from the sin of wittingly
neglecting the rites which are due to the dead. It is a
harsh code but one which lets a man know exactly what
his duty is and how to perform it.

An ancient sacrifice can best be imagined by looking
at pictures—such as the wall-paintings in the house of
the Vettii at Pompeii. There are also several sculptures
which portray the key stages of the ritual, and perhaps
the most vivid representation is a carving from Milan
(see plate I). The sacrificer stands facing forwards, with
his toga drawn over his head, at the right-hand side of a
low tripod altar fire. Behind him a flute-player pipes
busily and an attendant holds a box full of incense to
put on the fire. At the left of the altar a *victimarius*
holds by the throat a tiny steer which looks eagerly and
cheerfully at the flames on the altar.

Sacrifice was part of the Roman way of life. It was not always on the grand scale; many of the most devout sacrifices were of cakes or very small animals. But from childhood the Roman would have been brought up, in the circle of his family and in the wider sphere of public religion with its annual festivals and special ceremonies, to accept the idea that such offerings were acceptable to the gods. A little poem by Martial (X, 92) captures the spirit entirely. Martial has sold his country estate to a man called Marius and he is anxious that the new owner should look after the holy places which had meant so much to him—the woods sacred to Flora and the Fauni, the shrines of Diana and Mars, and, above all, the altars of Jupiter and Silvanus, constructed by the farm-manager's unskilled hands and 'which were often stained with the blood of a lamb or a kid'. Horace's attitude to the fountain of Bandusia was not a regrettable lapse from good taste. It was the behaviour of a normal, religious man.

4

Divination

One for sorrow,
Two for joy,
Three for a girl,
Four for a boy.

THE belief that natural phenomena reveal the will of
the gods or foretell the future is very old. Religion is
concerned with establishing the right relationship with
the gods, inducing the gods to co-operate in the successful operation of the processes of life, and this requires
some form of two-way communication. You have to
know whether your prayers and your sacrifices are
acceptable or not; otherwise, like a one-sided telephone
conversation, you might as well not make them at all.
The ultimate proof is, of course, if they are answered,
but most people have not been content with such a hit-
or-miss procedure. Instead they have looked for signs in
the stars, in cherry-stones, in tea-leaves, in glass-balls
and in a thousand other media. At the same time a terrifying event such as an earthquake or a flood, which cannot be explained readily in terms of available scientific
laws, is looked on as the direct intervention of a supernatural power in the running of the world. Such events
might be meaningless and random, but it is less disturbing to believe that they are sent for a purpose. The
search for knowledge, after all, is based on the assumption that the world is rational. Man's task is to interpret
the event, to discover what that purpose is.

These two beliefs, the belief that divine will could be
ascertained and the belief that the gods sent signs in the
form of extraordinary phenomena, were an integral part
of Roman religion. They received strong intellectual
backing in the Augustan age from the spread of Stoicism

and, to a lesser extent, from astrological theories introduced from the East. Stoicism held that the universe
was composed of a fiery spirit which permeated everything (human beings were part of it just as much as
birds or cows) and that this rational spirit ordained and
controlled everything which happened. Because it was
present in all creatures, there was a common understanding between the different parts of the universe
which caused one event to be reflected in another.
Hence there was nothing implausible about supposing
'that the divine providence could be reproduced in a
sheep's liver or the flight of birds'. One of the most en-
lightened Stoics, Epictetus, only qualified his belief in
divination, or the art of ascertaining the will of heaven
through signs, by advising people also to be influenced
in their actions by a sense of duty. There is a good
illustration of this Stoic attitude in Apuleius' *Apology*
(43) when he describes how a young and innocent boy
can be put into a trance by music or fumes so that he
'forgets the present and returns to his own nature which
is immortal and divine and so can by a kind of instinct
foretell the future'.

Astrology spread from Babylonia and Egypt to Italy
in the second century B.C. and soon gained a strong hold
over credulous minds. In its most rigorous form, astrology was incompatible with religion and divination
because it held that everything which happened, human
actions and natural phenomena alike, depended on the
revolutions of the heavenly bodies, and since *these* were
governed by an inflexible necessity everything was pre-
destined and determined. Suetonius says that the
emperor Tiberius was 'careless about the gods and
religion because he was addicted to astrology and
believed that everything was ruled by fate' (*Tiberius*
69). As Vettius Valens put it: 'It is impossible for any
man by prayers and sacrifice to overcome what is fixed
from the beginning and to alter it to his taste; what has
been assigned to us will happen without our praying for
it, what is not fated will not happen for our prayers.'
But for most people the stars were not so mechanical.

If they controlled and foreshadowed the future course
of events, they did so because the gods had willed it to
be so. To learn what the stars had in store was only to
discover what the gods intended. Popular astrology
was enormously fashionable under the early Empire, as
a lengthy poem on the subject by Manilius indicates and
as Tacitus states when he comments that astrologers, 'a
breed of men who betray the powerful and deceive the
hopeful, were constantly being banned from Rome and
were constantly to be found there' (*Histories* I, 22).
Almost every excavation in Italy unearths hundreds of
astrological amulets, charms and such like.

Stoicism and astrology, then, helped to maintain faith
in the traditional methods of divination practised at
Rome, despite the scepticism of men like Cicero who,
although himself an augur, laboriously compiled a work
(*On divination*) to disprove the possibility of it. For-
tunately official divination never became disreputable:
it never descended to quack horoscopes. This was partly
because it had been developed to provide answers to
the question, 'Is this course of action approved by the
gods?' or 'What does this sign tell us about the gods'
will?' rather than 'What will happen tomorrow?' or
'Who will win the Derby?' and partly because its rules
and interpretations were carefully formalised (the *ius
augurale*) and there was only a limited number of recognised officials who might be consulted about them. And
these officials only had a consultative role; they were
never able to initiate action or to use their powers and
knowledge to invoke the gods on their own account.
Just as it was not a priest but the individual citizen on
behalf of himself and his family and the magistrates on
behalf of the state as a whole who approached the gods
by prayer and sacrifice to secure their co-operation, so it
was the responsibility of the individual in private life
and the magistrates in public affairs to discover if that
co-operation was being secured and, if not, what the will
of the gods was. The augurs and other professionals were
there to advise and explain, not to dictate.

There were two main classes of signs by which the

gods made their will known, those which were deliberately solicited before a course of action was undertaken
(*impetrativa*) and those which were sent unasked
(*oblativa*). These applied equally in public and private
life, but the evidence is so much fuller about public
divination that it is worth seeing in detail how it worked
and then relating it to the scattered details which we
have about private practice.

Before any major decision of state such as the holding
of an assembly, the declaration of war or the passing of
a law, the will of heaven had to be ascertained. When
two or three magistrates of different ranks were present
(e.g. a consul, a praetor, and an aedile), only the
superior magistrate could ask for a sign from heaven.
Since the standard sign came from the observation of
birds, a magistrate who was empowered to ask for a sign
was said to have the auspices (*auspicia*, which literally
means bird-watching), and he would take his seat in the
open and designate a quarter of the sky in which he
would watch for a sign. In Rome there was a special site
(the *auguraculum*) on the Capitol which was reserved
for the purpose and the magistrate would be accompanied by one of the college of fifteen augurs, distinguished public figures like himself, who pronounced
the ceremonial formula for designating the quarter of
the sky and would interpret, blind-folded, any signs
which the magistrate reported. The practice was regarded so seriously that when in 99 B.C. T. Claudius
Centumalus built a house which obstructed the view
from the *auguraculum* he was forced to pull it down.
Outside Rome the whole ritual might have to be undertaken by the magistrate single-handed if there was no
augur present. He watched chiefly for birds, observing
their flight and their song. The raven, the crow and the
owl were supposed to give their sign by singing (*oscines*),
the eagle and the vulture by flying (*alites*). Pitch, intona-
tion and frequency determined whether the sign of the
oscines was good or bad, whereas speed, direction,
number and height were important for finding the
meaning of the *alites*. The exact interpretation was very

III Roman calendar: fragment of the *Fasti Caeretani* in the Museo Capitolino, Rome

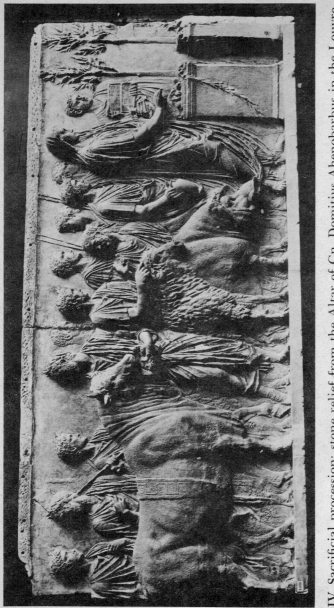

IV Sacrificial procession: stone relief from the Altar of Cn. Domitius Ahenobarbus in the Louvre

complicated and cannot now be reconstructed. Much evidently depended upon the time of day and the season of the year, but disputes such as that between Remus who saw six vultures first and Romulus who saw twelve shortly afterwards (Livy I, 7, 1), could obviously arise if the magistrates and his advisers were not thoroughly agreed on what sign they wanted to see. A later development was to study how birds ate (*ex tripudiis*). Any bird would do (according to Cicero, *On divination* II, 34) but in practice special chickens were kept for the purpose by licensed handlers (*pullarii*). They were much used on military expeditions when wild birds might not be around and a quick answer was needed. To consult them, the cage was opened and a piece of cake thrown in front of it. It was a bad sign if they declined to come out and eat it, or flew away, or flapped their wings and cackled, while it was a favourable omen if they tried to gobble it up and bits fell from their beaks. Opinions varied as to their reliability. In the First Punic War Ap. Claudius Pulcher threw the sacred chickens into the Tiber with a brusque 'Well, let them drink,' when they declined to eat as requested, thereby jeopardising the expedition on which he had set his heart. The expedition proved disastrous. They were taken seriously even in Cicero's day, two hundred years later. In 46 B.C. Cicero wrote cautiously to a brother-augur, A. Caecina, a distinguished member of an old Etruscan family, who had been exiled for his support of Pompey. He predicted that Caesar would pardon Caecina, 'not from the flight of birds or the favourable singing of birds, as in our profession, nor from crumbs that fall from the chickens' beaks, but I have other signs that I watch for—Caesar's character; not that mine are more reliable than the traditional signs but they are less ambiguous, less easily mistaken'. Unlike Cicero, Caecina obviously had faith in augury which Cicero was too polite to question openly in writing to him. Caecina was not alone. Suetonius records that Augustus believed implicitly in the auspices and there were many educated Romans who did so too.

The use of birds, which is common in many civilisations, is not wholly arbitrary or irrational. Swallows, for instance, do forecast the approach of rain because the change in barometric pressure and humidity keeps the insects which they eat close to the ground. The sudden arrival of winter-thrushes from the north is often the harbinger of a cold spell. When divination was adopted in Rome, the Romans were still farmers who were quick to profit from any practical warnings which birds or animals could give them.

Another method of ascertaining the will of the gods was to watch for lightning rather than birds. Lightning was, *par excellence*, the prerogative of Jupiter and, therefore, the most authoritative sign of all. The place where lightning struck was immediately declared holy, because it seemed that Jupiter had claimed it for himself. The area, called *bidental*, was enclosed and sacrifices and prayers were made there. When Anchises refused to leave Troy, a miraculous fire broke out on his grandson's head. To ascertain whether this was a favourable omen, or not, he asked Jupiter to give him a sign. Jupiter obliged with a sudden peal of thunder on the left and a flash of lightning which ran from the roofs of Troy to the forest of Ida. Anchises knew that Jupiter did not wish him to stay behind (Virgil, *Aeneid* II, 682–98). The appearance of lightning to a magistrate taking the auspices before a public assembly was always enough to prevent any meeting for that day, but, particularly in sunlight, it is much easier to imagine that you have seen a glint of lightning than to convince people of a non-existent flight of birds. Auspices of lightning were, therefore, peculiarly liable to abuse. Bibulus, the consul of 59 B.C., had only to announce that he was going 'to watch the sky' (*servare de caelo*), i.e. look for signs of the gods' will, for public business to be indefinitely suspended. It was an accepted fact that if he looked for lightning hard enough he would find it. Thirty years later it had become an automatic matter of course for a magistrate, when he took the auspices on entering office, to 'see lightning' on his left. It was a meaningless symbol of good luck. Thunder was also studied. There survives, at third hand, a calendar which gives the significance of thunder-claps on each day of the year. Thus if it thunders on 3 December a shortage of fish will make people eat meat; if it thunders on 19 August, women and slaves will commit murder.

The gods could not only be consulted. They might make their will known spontaneously by sending signs. Any miraculous event was evidence of divine intention and required the most careful elucidation. Roman history is full of such portents or prodigies, as they were called. If the gods showed that they were unwilling to co-operate, there was cause for profound anxiety. The only events that were felt to be worth recording in historical chronicles were the occasions when the gods had signified their displeasure and the measures that were taken in consequence to conciliate them.

It is, then, no accident that the only documentary sources for early Roman history were the chronicles of the *pontifices* which preserved notices of prodigies and other religious occurrences. History to the Romans was the story of divine intervention in the affairs of men. Livy states that prodigies were less frequently reported in his day because people were more 'negligent' about the gods, but he regarded this as a sign of decadence and a cause of contemporary troubles which he at least was not going to abet. He took care to fill his *History* with detailed lists of the signs which the gods sent. The variety of these signs is best appreciated from the record of a particular year (169 B.C.): 'At Anagnia a torch was seen in the sky and a cow talked. At Menturnae the sky seemed to be on fire. At Reate it rained stones. At Cumae the statue of Apollo wept for three days and three nights. In Rome a crested snake was seen in the temple of Fortuna, a palm-tree grew in the forecourt of the temple of Primigenia Fortuna, and it rained with blood. A further prodigy, which was not officially recognised, occurred at Fregellae when a spear blazed for more than two hours without being consumed' (Livy XLIII, 13, 3–7). The signs which were given to

Pompey's army before the battle of Pharsalus should have
discouraged them. Lucan reports that 'the whole sky set
itself against their march: the troops were bombarded
with thunderbolts, fire-balls and meteors: the standards
could not be pulled from the earth and were made so
heavy by the swarms of bees that settled on them that
the standard-bearers could not lift them: they even
seemed to weep tears at the prospect before them. The
bull that was to be sacrificed kicked the altar over and
ran away and no replacement for it could be found in
time.' No wonder that the soldiers quaked with fear
(*Pharsalia* VII, 151–87). Even Tacitus, one of the most
sceptical of Roman writers, tells how on the day that the
great battle of Bedriacum was fought in A.D. 69, a strange
bird settled in a wood near Regium Lepidum and could
not be scared away until Otho, the defeated emperor,
killed himself, whereupon it vanished. He adds, 'It is
undignified for a historian to invent or collect marvels
but I would not presume to discredit the truth of this
apparition,' just as he was evidently convinced by the
prodigy of a flock of ill-omened birds which darkened
the sky when Vitellius contemplated fighting at Mevania
some months later (*Histories* II, 50; III, 56).

Such signs were observed and studied by most
Romans, and, although it is not always easy to tell where
mere superstition (e.g. a black cat crossing the road)
begins and divination ends, we should recognise that
the Romans genuinely believed that the gods made their
meaning known by signs. Few people were as callous as
the elder Marcellus, an augur, who always travelled on
campaign in a litter with the blinds drawn so that he
should not see any signs. The majority would have
shared Augustus' attitude who was much moved when
a dying oak-tree revived on his arrival at the island of
Capri.

One form of omen to which the Romans attached
particular importance was the interpretation of chance
remarks. When they were debating whether or not to
move the capital from Rome after the destruction of
the city by the Gauls (*c.* 386 B.C.) a company of soldiers

happened to halt in the market-place on the orders of
their officer, 'Let's stop here.' The words were taken to
be divinely inspired and to mean that the Romans
should not move from Rome. At a later period the
consul L. Paullus was selected to conduct the war
against the Macedonian king Perseus. When he came
home in the evening to tell his family the news, he was
met by his little daughter in tears, crying that her pet
dog called 'The Persian' had died. Paullus welcomed
the omen. The belief was still strong under the later
Republic. Pompey, on the run after the battle of Pharsalus, felt that his last hope was gone when he was told
that a friendly-looking settlement which he sighted from
his ship was called 'Kingsdown'.

The bewildering variety of signs and portents needed
authoritative interpretation. In cases where a magistrate deliberately sought the will of heaven on a particular issue the problem was relatively straightforward.
He had asked the gods for a 'yes' or 'no' answer, and
any sign that was given must mean one or the other.
When in doubt he would seek the advice of an augur.
By the time of Augustus there was a considerable
volume of literature on the meaning and interpretation
of auspices. In addition to the surviving *On divination*
by Cicero, we hear of works of augural lore written by
his contemporaries A. Caecina, M. Massalla (the consul
of 53 B.C.), Ap. Claudius (his predecessor as governor of
Cilicia), and, above all, a great scholar Nigidius Figulus
who wrote on private augury. Although the methods of
the augurs were supposed to be secret, these books will
have provided a store of traditional interpretations
which turned augury into an elaborate and well-
organised science.

The unsolicited signs (*oblativa*), however, were more
troublesome because, instead of merely giving negative
or affirmative answers to questions, the gods were using
them as a language to communicate positive messages of
their own, as they drove the natives by 'celestial prodigies' to build a mound to Palinurus and make sacrifice
at it (Virgil, *Aeneid* VI, 378). It was not always easy to

understand what the gods were talking about. If a sign came, unasked, to a magistrate, it was up to him to decide whether to take notice of it or not. If it came to an augur and he announced it (*nuntiatio*), it had to be respected. If it came to a private citizen, he reported it to the *pontifices*, who were then responsible for accepting or ignoring it. Certain sorts of signs, which were often reported, such as talking cows or blood-storms, had acquired a conventional meaning which did not need great thought to understand. The *pontifices* looked at past examples and took whatever therapeutic action had been recommended then. If they were in doubt about the precise significance of a prodigy, they could get a ruling from the augurs, but, if it had not occurred previously, they would have no guidance how to deal with it. The augurs, for instance, might rule that the gods were angry about something but, if there were no precedents, how were the *pontifices* to decide what steps should be taken for appeasing them?

When the ordinary measures and remedies failed, they advised the Senate to consult the Sibylline Books. These books, traditionally a collection of oracles purchased from a prophetic woman (Sibyl) by the last King of Rome, had been kept in a stone-chest underground in the temple of Jupiter on the Capitol, but they were burnt in 82 B.C. in a fire which destroyed the temple and were replaced by a new collection assembled from various places in Italy, Greece and the East. The new books, consisting of verse-oracles written in Greek, which were subsequently recopied and rehoused in two gold chests in the temple of Apollo on the Palatine by Augustus, were in the charge of a college of fifteen men (*quindecimviri*) who alone had the right of consulting them. Like the augurs and the *pontifices*, the *quindecimviri* were not professional priests but public men (Tacitus, no priest, was one) and it was a social distinction to be elected to the college. On a motion passed by the Senate, the *quindecimviri* would see what the Sibylline books had to say. We do not know the exact process. The leaves of the books may have been loose and the *quindecimviri* may have drawn one at random and read it. The authority of the Sibylline books was, however, so great that its recommendations were almost always followed. Historically they were responsible for the introduction of many new, especially Greek, cults—a policy which was in many ways far-sighted since the novelty of the cults often distracted and satisfied frightened emotions at a time of crisis. For instance in 400 B.C. an unprecedentedly severe winter, during which the roads were blocked and the Tiber frozen, was followed by a hot, sickly summer. This happened at one of the worst moments of the war against Veii and drove the Romans to despair. The Sibylline books were consulted and recommended that the right relationship with the gods (the *pax deorum*) could only be restored by introducing a completely new ritual, the display of statues of the gods reclining on couches at meals (*lectisternia*). The spectacle was certainly guaranteed to take the minds of the Romans off other things. The prestige of the Sibylline books lasted throughout the classical period. In 56 B.C. they unambiguously declared against an army being employed in Egypt and so prevented Pompey from achieving the military command which he wanted. Later they provided some convenient arithmetic for Augustus to hold the Secular Games (commemorating a century (*saeculum*) in the life of Rome) in 17 B.C. They were undoubtedly liable to political 'inspiration' or manipulation, but this did not give the same offence to the Romans as it does to us because religion, as has been seen, was concerned less with personal integrity than with public success. If the measures proposed and adopted worked, this was in itself the proof of religious efficacy.

The same distinction between solicited and unsolicited signs extended to private affairs. Cicero says that even in private life no important step was taken without ascertaining the will of heaven. By Augustus' time it is doubtful whether this precaution was observed by most people, although Augustus himself was very punctilious. Before any long journey, for instance, he noticed whether there had been a heavy dew or not; if there had been, it meant that the gods favoured his journey and would give him a speedy and safe return. Only in marriage (which is always a very conservative institution) were auspices regularly taken by observing the flight of birds, as Catullus means when he says that Julia is being wedded to Manlius Torquatus 'with the blessing of a bird' (61, 19–20 *cum bona alite*). It is likely that the other great event in the life of the family, the coming of age of a son, which was symbolised by his putting on grown-up clothes for the first time (the *toga virilis*), was also safeguarded in this way. The head of the family would in such cases be responsible for observing the omen and interpreting it. But although we do not hear much about formal divination by private individuals, Horace gives us a strong impression that it must still have been quite widespread: 'whereas others,' he says (*Odes* III, 27, 1), 'attempt to predict the outcome of their journeys by the cry of the owl or the sight of a wild wolf running down from the fields of Lanuvium or the appearance of a pregnant dog or fox, and others are deterred by a snake that crosses their path and frightens their horses or by the flight of a woodpecker or a crow, I have only to look at the threatening waves to know the dangers that my mistress is running if she goes on this voyage'.

Birds, however, are not of so much importance in the daily life of a townsman as they are to a countryman and part of the decline in the use of auspices from birds in private affairs must have been due to the urban environment in which most Romans of Augustus' time lived. They were to a large extent replaced by two other media for ascertaining the will of the gods. The main sanction of prayer, the method used to persuade the gods to fulfil prayer, was sacrifice and in sacrifice it was all-important that the offering should be perfect and acceptable. The test of this was its outward and inward appearance, but whereas many people are fair judges of the external points of a cow, most are amateurs when it comes to deciding whether the liver is in perfect order or not. A science of this specialised subject grew up. The temple priests were competent to decide on inspection whether the internal organs of a victim were satisfactory or not but, because the liver was such a vital organ and was, in Stoic theory, a microcosm of the working of the universe, it was believed that detailed examination could see in it a more intricate pattern of what the gods intended.

The science was one cultivated by the Etruscans and it was from Etruria that the real experts, *haruspices* as they were called, always came. The *haruspices* were never an official priesthood at Rome; they never held the authority and status of augurs or *pontifices* and originally no Roman citizen could be a *haruspex*, although this was no longer true in Cicero's day. Nevertheless, when a doubtful point of interpretation of a liver arose in a private or a public sacrifice the recognised *haruspices* (who under the Empire formed a society of sixty members) were on hand to give (for a fee) their opinion. (A relief from the Louvre (see plate II) portrays the scene after an animal has been killed, as the *haruspex* prepares to examine the entrails.) There was, in addition, a large body of unofficial *haruspices* who had picked up a smattering of the subject. Most emperors never stirred without a *haruspex* on their staff, although even that did not always save them. The emperor Vitellius' *haruspex*, a man named Umbricius, warned him that the entrails revealed a dangerous plot in the palace: Vitellius was murdered the same day. The details of the science cannot now be reconstructed, but there is preserved a bronze model of a liver, found at Piacenza, which must have been used as a model for instruction or practice. 'It is divided into two halves, each containing on its margin eight regions and marked on the back with "of the Sun" and "of the Moon" respectively, and meaning probably day and night' (Weinstock, *Journal of Roman Studies* 36 (1946), p. 121). These sixteen regions correspond with the sixteen divisions into which the Etruscans divided the heavens, and indicate the correlation between the cosmic and the terrestrial life. Inside these 'marginal regions are inner segments, sixteen on the day-side and eight on the night-side'. Each of the forty divisions bears the name of a divinity who presumably controls it. One can assume that some abnormality found in a real liver could be checked against the model and interpreted as meaning that the relevant god was thereby asserting his will.

Although the *haruspices* were primarily concerned with the inspection of livers (their name perhaps means 'gut-gazers' as H. J. Rose translated it), they were also approached for their opinions on other divine manifestations, such as earthquakes. They were, for example, invited in 56 B.C. to explain certain mysterious noises and reported that the gods were displeased at the profanation of certain rites. This was seized on by Clodius as a reference to the rebuilding of Cicero's home, on his return from exile, on land which had been deliberately consecrated. Whatever the political motives of their judgement, Cicero was obliged to treat their findings sufficiently seriously to devote a long and vitriolic speech (*On the Answers of the Haruspices*) to rebutting Clodius.

The *haruspices* played a prominent part in Roman religious life, even before the emperor Claudius patronised them and took steps to ensure that there should be steady recruitment to their ranks from Etruscan families. Many prominent people at all periods consulted them. The tribune C. Gracchus seems to have had a *haruspex* in regular attendance as part of his household (Valerius Maximus IX, 12, 6) and nearly two hundred years later the famous advocate and senator M. Aquilius Regulus frequently sought their advice. The younger Pliny tells the story of how Regulus acquired a large legacy by assuring a sick woman that the conjunction of the stars at her birth proved that she was not going to die yet and confirming this by getting a *haruspex* whom he often consulted to report that the entrails at a sacrifice, which he made specially on her behalf, pointed to the same conclusion. The woman believed him, altered her will in his favour, and promptly died. Juvenal, too, is full of anecdotes about the fashionable

men and women who flocked to them for expensive
advice.

Yet opinion was deeply divided about their value.
Cicero, of course, discredited the whole business,
quoting a remark of the elder Cato who wondered how
one *haruspex* could look at another without laughing,
and Columella, who wrote on agricultural subjects
under the early Empire, attacks 'the *haruspices* and
soothsayers who fleece the ignorant in return for idle
superstitions'. Even more celebrated was Hannibal's
retort when King Prusias refused to allow him to begin
a battle because the entrails were unfavourable: 'Do you
put more faith in a slice of veal than in an old general?'
But such rational ridicule did not carry the day. People
continued to consult the *haruspices* so widely that the
emperor Tiberius was forced to regulate the profession
and to insist that all consultations should be held in
public before witnesses in order to minimise the possi-
bilities of fraud. And they continued to enjoy intellectual backing. The practice of divination from the liver
was patiently defended by the philosopher Epictetus. It
remained one of the principal forms of private augury.

The other common form was based on the interpretation of dreams. Dreams have always seemed uncanny
and in many civilisations they have been regarded as a
means of communication from the supernatural or the
divine. They also have a curious knack of foretelling the
future. Although the philosophical theory behind J. W.
Dunne's *Experiment with Time* may not be acceptable,
he accumulated a fascinating collection of authenticated
pre-cognitive dreams (i.e. dreams that record events
which subsequently occur) which suggests that the
ancient belief in the value of dreams does have a real
basis in experience. Even the elder Pliny, who was not
impressed by most of the methods used to anticipate the
future, was persuaded that dreams could be significant.
He himself investigated the case of a soldier, suffering
from the poisonous effects of a dog-bite, who was cured
by applying a remedy revealed in a dream by his mother
absent in Spain. Pliny's contemporaries required less

persuasion to accept the truth of Homer's assertion that dreams are sent by Zeus (*Iliad* I, 63). Augustus had been saved at Philippi by a timely dream which advised him not to stay sick in his tent. The dream proved well-founded, for the camp was surprised and his tent cut to pieces. From then on, if not earlier, he paid the most careful attention to dreams even when they led him into ridiculous situations such as taking his stand as a beggar in the streets of Rome one day each year and holding out his hand for alms from the passers-by. Dreams are prominent both in Livy and in Virgil. If it is less easy to be sure how far Virgil believed in 'them himself because they were part of the epic machinery inherited from Homer, Livy certainly seems to have accepted them as trustingly as Augustus. He tells, for instance, of T. Latinius who saw a dream in which Jupiter said that he disapproved of the prelude-dancer who opened the great games and told Latinius to report his displeasure to the magistrates. Latinius was a mere plebeian and, although a devout believer, he was scared to approach such remote dignitaries as the consuls. He did nothing about it until a series of personal disasters and repeated dreams drove him in extremities to brave the Senate and tell them his story. The Senate at once took note of the matter and ordered the games to be repeated. The story was an old one but Livy's version assumes the credibility of dreams; there is nothing sceptical or apologetic about it.

There is little direct evidence of how far people's day-to-day life was governed by dreams, but, apart from anecdotes, such as that in Pliny's letters about the historian Suetonius trying to put off a civil case in which he and Pliny were involved because of a bad dream, there are two indications that suggest that reliance on dreams was very widespread indeed. Lucretius devotes much space in his fourth book to giving a scientific explanation of dreams as material films or images which produce sensation in the same way that sight does. His argument is designed to remove the mystery from dreams which would otherwise tempt men to think of them as divine inspirations. The persistence with which he returns to the subject shows the strength of the superstitions about dreams which he was attacking. Secondly, interpreters of dreams clearly did a flourishing trade under the late Republic and early Empire. There were even handbooks which collected significant dreams and their interpretations. One example of this literature, from a later period, survives: it is by Artemidorus of Ephesus who lived at Rome *c*. A.D. 150. A single quotation is sufficient to give the character of the whole. 'If you dream of a house on fire and it burns with pure flames but does not collapse, it means wealth if you are poor, power if you are rich. But if it is a smoky fire, which destroys the house and brings it down in ruins, it is bad for everyone connected with the house and means the ruin of the owner. If only a part of the house is destroyed, it depends on which part is involved: if it is the bedroom, it means disaster for the wife (or, if there is no wife, for the master of the house); if it is the men's room, it means disaster for all the men of the household; if it is the women's room, for all the women; if it is the store-rooms or the housekeeper's room, for the steward or the housekeeper.'

But even if individuals were influenced in their behaviour by dreams which they imagined to be communications from the gods, dreams never had an official place in religion, except when for a short period there was a precaution that anyone who had a dream concerned with the state should have it publicly proclaimed. It is clear why this was so. Dreams are inherently private and difficult to verify, and they cannot be genuinely produced to order, but religion has to satisfy continuing needs and to ascertain at any time what is the will of the gods. It is no good waiting for a dream to tell you whether to set out on an expedition or not if, like Augustus (so Suetonius says), you only have dreams in the spring.

5

The Religious Year

NATURE is regular. Day in, day out, year in, year out, life goes on. The seeds grow, the crops ripen, the harvest is gathered. Winter gives place to summer, sunshine to rain. In all this process the Romans believed that the gods were active. Therefore, although in sudden crises and emergencies both the state and individuals alike might turn to the gods with special prayers and sacrifices, it was also necessary to have a regular schedule for ensuring that all the gods were duly conciliated every year. In order to get some idea of that religious year it will help to look first at the cults which were undertaken by or on behalf of the people as a whole and then to examine the private routine of individuals or groups.

As in the Christian year some feasts are (within limits) movable, such as Easter, while others, such as Christmas, are fixed, so the Romans had from very early times worked out a calendar which gave the dates of all the fixed festivals of the different gods (*feriae stativae*) and thus indicated the periods within which the few movable festivals (*feriae conceptivae*) could be placed each year. Although this calendar satisfactorily settled the absolute *dates* of all the festivals, it suffered for centuries from a failure to reconcile a lunar year of 354 days with a solar year of $365\frac{1}{4}$ days, with the result that incompetent mathematics or political wangling often led to the winter festivals being celebrated in mid-summer. In 190 B.C. an eclipse, which really occurred (by our calendar) on 14 March, was observed on 11 July. In 46 B.C., however, Julius Caesar, on expert advice, issued an improved calendar which is substantially the same as the calendar which we use today with months of thirty and thirty-one days and a leap-year every four years. Caesar's new calendar was generally made known by being displayed in public places throughout the Empire and

fragments of about forty copies of it survive inscribed
on stone. These copies enable us to reconstruct almost
exactly the religious year of the Romans. In addition
Ovid wrote a verse commentary, the *Fasti*, on the calendar, six books of which, dealing with January to June,
are preserved.

A glance at a picture of one of these calendars shows
how it gives the dates of the important festivals, just as
a modern calendar will give Saints' Days and the major
feast-days of the Church (see plate III). But there are
two other things to be noticed about it. Each day
throughout the year is marked with a letter beside it.
These letters tell what sort of a day it is, whether it is a
working day or a holiday. Thus N (= *nefastus*) indicated a day on which certain sorts of public business could
not be done. Most of these days marked N were set aside
for religious festivals concerned with the dead or with
purification. NP also denoted a holiday but differed
from N in that it seems to have marked the great public
festivals of the state. There were also eight days in
the year marked EN (*endotercisus*: 'cut in parts') which
were religious festivals in the morning and evening.
Such days were like Bank Holidays: civil law-suits could
not be heard, the official assemblies of the people could
not be convened, some public business could not be
transacted. But there was not a complete shut-down.
Schools and markets remained open, the Senate could
meet, criminal cases could be heard and, as Cicero
makes clear at the beginning of his speech *In defence of
Caelius*, a threat to law and order or a breach of the
peace could be dealt with on them. In the time of
Augustus there were about a hundred and fifteen such
days a year—over a third of the whole year. Days marked
F (*fastus*) were ordinary working days, while C (*comi-
tialis*) implied that assemblies (and other legal sessions)
could properly be held.

The second notable feature about the calendar is the
way in which each month was subdivided. For ordinary
civil purposes the Romans had a week of eight days
(marked on some calendars A–H) with a market-day

(*nundinae*) every eighth day, but for religious purposes there were three key points in the month; the Kalends or first of the month (so called because, in early times before the standard calendar was fixed, the *pontifex* 'called' out the first day of the month when he first observed the crescent of the new moon); the Nones, which varied between the fifth and the seventh day of the month and originally corresponded to the first quarter of the moon; and the Ides, the thirteenth or fifteenth day, which corresponded to the full moon. The Kalends were sacred to Juno, most of whose festivals fall on the first day of the month, the Ides were sacred to Jupiter (e.g. the festival of Jupiter Optimus Maximus on the Capitol was celebrated on the Ides of September), while on the Nones one of the leading priests (the *rex sacrorum*: see p. 109) used to announce the dates of any of the movable festivals to be held in the course of the month.

These official calendars gave Romans the essential time-table for the regular worship of their gods. But most families will also have had small calendars in their own homes which marked important dates and festivals. The enterprising Trimalchio had two boards put up on either side of his door which served as a diary to remind him when he was due to go out for dinner and also to distinguish the lucky from the unlucky days of the year (Petronius, *Satyricon* 30). We also hear of several Romans marking a happy day on their calendars with a white stone or mark and putting a black mark against a disastrous or bad day (Pliny, *Natural History* VII, 40). Catullus (107, 6) and Horace (*Odes* I, 36, 10) both commemorated their lucky days in this way.

So it is reasonable to believe that most people were aware of the dates of the annual festivals which were intended to secure the goodwill of the different gods on whose continuing favour they depended. But this does not mean that the average Roman actually attended any religious ceremony on these days. For one thing the highly conservative character of the religious calendar meant that many of the major festivals were concerned with primitive agricultural deities who no longer had any obvious relevance to the spiritual needs of a busy, commercial city. Furthermore the efficacy of a religious ceremony depended simply upon the ritual being properly carried out; it did not require the temples to be packed with devout congregations. The purpose of week-day evensong in a Cathedral is not to be judged by the size of the attendance. So many of the festivals, which must have meant much to the Rome of the Kings, passed almost unnoticed by the Romans of Augustus' day. There were some, however, which did still attract general attention and it is worth going through month by month to see the chief land-marks in the religious life of the city. Many festivals which were of great significance for the history of Roman religion or which are of antiquarian interest have been omitted and only those which seemed to have meant something in the life of the people have been included.

· Originally the year had started in March, as one can see from the character of the festivals at the beginning of that month, but at some early time the New Year had been put back, for administrative reasons, to 1 January and this is the date which was kept by Julius Caesar in his revised calendar. As a result January, the month of Janus, the god of entrances, is curiously lacking in important or long-established festivals. The one event which did arouse interest was the sacrifice performed by the incoming consuls on 1 January and this, because it was instituted relatively late, does not even figure in the calendar which marks 1 January as F, a normal working day. But on that day, as Ovid vividly imagines as he writes from exile to congratulate Sex. Pompeius on his election to the consulship, the consuls put on their purple-bordered togas for the first time and set out from their homes, preceded by the lictors, in a solemn procession of friends, clients and acquaintances up the Sacred Way to the Capitol. Ovid pictures the temple so densely crowded that spectators are crushed and hurt as they try to see what is going on (*Letters from Pontus* IV, 4, 25*ff*.). White bulls were sacrificed to Jupiter in payment of the vows for the safety of the Roman state which their predecessors had made the previous January, and fresh vows were made for the coming year. Then the consuls sat for the first time on their official ivory chairs (*sella curulis*), which were placed in the open in front of the temple, and received the cheers and greetings of the populace, before processing down the hill again to preside over a meeting of the Senate. On a fine day it must have been a colourful and impressive spectacle.

The other festival which was still generally celebrated in Dionysius of Halicarnassus' day (*Roman Antiquities* IV, 14) was the Compitalia. This also was not mentioned in the calendar since it was a movable feast, held on a date fixed by the city praetor some time early in January. It was originally an agricultural festival. The point at which four small-holdings or estates met was called a *compitum* and at it a small shrine was erected, open in all four directions so that the spirit that presided over each farm (*Lar*: see below p. 101) could come and go freely. Four small altars were placed round it. At the Compitalia (which marked the end of the agricultural year), the farmers would hang up a plough on the shrine and also a woollen doll for every free person in the household and a woollen ball for every slave. The following day a sacrifice would be performed at the altar and everybody would have a holiday. The aim of the ceremony was clearly to reinvigorate the whole farm for the work that lay in the months ahead and it remained such a strong custom in the country that Cicero in 50 B.C. was reluctant to visit his Alban estate on the day of the Compitalia because of the inconvenience which it would cause to his domestic staff (*Letters to Atticus* VII, 7, 3).

In the city blocks of houses took the place of farms, and the chapels were set up at cross-roads, like wayside shrines in Catholic countries today. The inhabitants of each block were organised under a president who was responsible for arranging the formal sacrifice (of a hen) and the subsequent festivities which often took the form

of impromptu plays, dances or games in the open air
at the intersection of the streets. Since slaves as well as
free people were traditionally allowed to share in the
festival, which lasted for three days, it was usually a noisy
and riotous affair. It also lent itself to political exploita-
tion. The blocks of houses provided the one local unit
in ancient Rome which, like a parish, could readily be
organised through their presidents for political purposes
and in the late Republic they often staged intimidating
demonstrations. Consequently the Compitalia were
twice suppressed (in 64 B.C. and again in 45 B.C. after
they had been restored in 58 B.C.), but Augustus felt
strong enough to revive the Compitalia because it was
a festival which encouraged a sense of identity among all
the inhabitants of an area and this, in such a huge and
heterogeneous place as Rome, was a valuable thing.
Rome, like London, was a city in which there were no
neighbours, 'only men'.

February was—and is—a dreary month. It takes its
name from *februum*, which means an instrument of
purification, and the two chief festivals of the month,
the Parentalia and the Lupercalia, are in a wide sense
concerned with purification, by securing the repose of
the dead and promoting future fertility. The Romans
were much concerned about the welfare of the dead.
Besides the Parentalia, which lasted from 13 to 24
February, a period during which the temples were
closed and no marriages could be celebrated, there was
another and older festival of the dead in May, the
Lemuria (p. 85), and in domestic worship the family
dead, the Lares, were constantly conciliated (p. 101). But
the Parentalia was devoted particularly to the care of
dead parents. The old belief was that the spirits of the
deceased remained in a state of semi-existence in the
tomb or near the ashes of its body. These spirits were
called by the all-embracing plural noun, *Manes*, a word
of uncertain meaning, perhaps either 'Powers' or 'Kindly
Ones'. It was widely held that the Manes required
regular feeding in order to be kept 'alive'. Hence it was
usual, when burying a corpse, to enclose a good meal

(*silicernium*) with it in the tomb. These funeral meals
have been found both in the most primitive burials in
Rome and also in the luxurious chamber-tombs of Caere
and Tarquinii. But the food had also to be renewed
annually or else the Manes would either waste miserably
away into nothingness or would become hungry and
restive and start plaguing the living. Ovid relates that
when someone once forgot to give the Manes food they
angrily emerged from their tombs and spread death and
destruction throughout the city (*Fasti* II, 546). So it was
the duty of every Roman on the anniversary of the
deaths of his father and mother to ensure that they were
well-supplied for the following year. The ceremony is
most graphically described by Virgil when he tells in the
fifth book of the *Aeneid* of the honours paid by Aeneas
to Anchises' grave (especially lines 49*ff*.). He and his
companions went in procession to the spot and there
poured libations of wine, milk and blood. Aeneas threw
purple flowers onto the tomb, while he solemnly spoke
a greeting to his father.

At Rome the procedure had become somewhat
standardised by the end of the Republic. Although most
people would no doubt keep the dates of their parents'
death as a special occasion, the ceremonies at the tombs
seem to have been confined to the conventional week of
the Parentalia, during which it was believed that the
spirits were closest to the world, and not to have been
performed on the actual anniversaries. Ovid implies
that, whatever most Romans may have thought about
survival after death, they did keep up the custom and
we should try to visualise all this week little groups of
mourners making their way through the streets of Rome
to the big cemeteries on the outskirts of the city, with
sprays of flowers and jugs of wine and milk in their
hands. The week ended with a day of family reunion,
Caristia or *Cara Cognatio*, 'Dear Acquaintance', on 22
February, when all the members of the family met in
one house for dinner. It was evidently a great social
gathering which remained an integral part of Roman
life in Ovid's day.

During the same week as the Parentalia there was held the most famous of all ancient festivals, the Lupercalia. It was one of the great popular diversions of Rome, and one that could all too easily get out of hand. We do not know the name of the god in whose honour it was held, we do not know its real origin and we do not know who or even how many people were officially involved, but we can reconstruct in some detail what happened. There was a small cave on the Palatine Hill, known as the Lupercal, where on 15 February every year two teams of young men, called *Luperci*, met. They sacrificed there goats and a dog—highly unusual victims in Roman sacrifices—and the two leaders of the teams, normally young aristocrats, were smeared on the forehead with blood from the victims which was then wiped off by a piece of wool dipped in milk. At that point they had to utter a loud laugh. The sacrifice was followed by a feast in the cave for the *Luperci* which, as Valerius Maximus reports (II, 2, 9), was often a drunken affair. At its end the two teams, dressed only in the skins of the slaughtered goats, emerged from the cave and ran a race along a course at the bottom of the Palatine Hill which was from time immemorial marked out by stones. This was the high spot of the festival and used to draw huge crowds to the Forum. As they ran they whipped any people that they met with thin strips of goat-skin—a ritual thought to promote fertility. In 44 B.C. Mark Antony was the leader of one of the teams of *Luperci*, using the occasion to stir up popular support for Caesar, and Shakespeare catches the attitude of the spectators thus:

> 'Stand directly in Antonius' way
> When he doth run his course—For our elders say
> The barren touched in this holy chase
> Shake off their sterile curse.'
>
> (*Julius Caesar* I, 2, 3–9)

But the religious significance of the ceremony was submerged for most people in sheer emotional excitement. The vast crowds, the eager suspense and the sight of the naked runners, all contributed to make it an unrestrained and wild occasion. Cicero is clearly embarrassed at having to explain away the fact that his young client, M. Caelius was a member of one of the teams of *Luperci*. They had a reputation for immorality which he was anxious to gloss over. Similarly Augustus had to enact that no adolescent should be allowed to take part in the ceremony because of the dubious goings-on. But it was a great event in the life of the city and survived as late as A.D. 494 when Pope Gelasius I abolished it and replaced it with the festival of the Purification of the Virgin Mary, a Christian purification taking over from a pagan one.

March, the month of Mars, always retained the primitive character which it had had when it was the first month of the year. The New Year, for the earliest inhabitants of Rome, had meant two things—the rebirth of the vegetable world and the opening of a new campaigning season—but it had lost much of its impact when Rome had got other people to grow her crops and fight her wars for her. Nonetheless the calendar for March preserved a succession of festivals to Mars, the god of war and the protector of growth, which continued to be celebrated quietly by the priest of Mars (*flamen Martialis*) and other responsible persons, long after they had ceased to be of concern to the ordinary Roman. On 1 March the sacred fire in the shrine of Vesta was relit (see p. 90), and the homes of the priests and other sacred buildings were decorated with fresh laurel branches (a tree sacred to Mars). On 14 March there was a feast of Mars, which involved horse-racing in the Campus Martius. The races, perhaps a survival of cavalry exercises, became a popular attraction in their own right, but the race-goers do not seem to have felt it necessary to pay their devotions to Mars first. On 23 March, also a feast of Mars, the sacred trumpets (*tubae*), originally used in war, were purified.

But while these festivals had become very esoteric, there was one March ceremonial which, like the Trooping of the Colour, caught the imagination of citizen and visitor alike. There were two teams of dancers, *Salii*, consisting of twelve young patrician nobles whose parents had to be still alive, chosen by co-option. Throughout the month of March they were to be seen in the streets and markets of Rome, dressed in their bright and outlandish uniform, dancing a strange war-dance and chanting an archaic song whose words were unintelligible even in Cicero's day. Dionysius of Hali-carnassus, a Greek who spent some years in Rome, was deeply impressed by this pageantry. The uniform of the *Salii* was probably that worn by soldiers hundreds of years before in the Bronze Age. It consisted of an em-broidered tunic, a bronze plate protecting the breast, a short red cloak (*trabea*), a sword and a conical bronze helmet (*apex*). On 1 March they went to the sanctuary of Mars which was part of the old Palace (*regia*) in the Forum, and took down twelve bronze shields (*ancilia*) shaped, like the famous Mycenaean shields, in a figure of eight. Legend said that one of these shields had once fallen from the sky on 1 March and that a blacksmith named Mamurius was divinely instructed to manu-facture another eleven, but it is likely that in fact they were survivals (or copies) of very primitive Bronze Age shields—a further proof of the antiquity of the whole ceremony. Then they danced through the streets, wear-ing the shields on their left arms or carrying them slung on a pole and banging them with a drum-stick. At various points they stopped and chanted their hymn. The route which they took was traditional and each night they halted at a special house in a different part of the city, where they stored their shields and settled down to a large and well-earned dinner. Horace, search-ing for a word to describe a slap-up banquet, picks on 'fit for the *Salii*' (*Saliaribus dapibus*; *Odes* I, 37, 2), and the emperor Claudius once left a dinner-party of his own because the food and drink looked better where the *Salii* were eating. The climax of this marathon dance was 19 March, a day known as Quinquatrus, yet another festival of Mars, when they performed in the very heart of the city (the *comitium*) in the presence of the *ponti-*

fices. It ended on 24 March when the shields were finally restored to the *regia*.

In the old days *Salii* were distinguished people. But in the late Republic their prestige seems to have diminished. This reflects the fact that the patricians as such were a depressed minority and also that it must have been a time-consuming and rather exposed business to be a *Salius*. Even if you happened to be out of Rome during the month of March, you were supposed to stop where you were and not make a journey of any kind (Livy XXXVII, 33, 7). However, the dances, as Varro tells us, went on and Cicero makes it clear that the dinners did not suffer, and when more settled conditions returned the *Salii* regained their former glory. It is some measure of the esteem in which they were held that the Senate decreed that Augustus' name should be included in their hymn. People would turn aside to watch and listen as the *Salii* went by.

Almost every country and civilisation has a holiday in the spring, when the warm, long days begin to come again and the poor can relax after the rigours of winter. The Easter holiday serves this purpose in Europe. In Rome its equivalent was the festival of Anna Perenna on 15 March, the first full moon of the old New Year. The name and nature of the goddess are both obscure, though obviously connected with the passage of the year (*annus*), and we do not know who sacrificed what to her, but Ovid has given us a charming picture of what happened on her day. Like the London crowd streaming out to Epsom Downs on Derby Day, the people of Rome poured out to the fields that bordered the river Tiber and picnicked in couples there, either in the open or in simple home-made tents. It was a day of coarse jokes and many drinks, for it was a readily believed superstition that you would live for as many years as you could drink tumblers of wine. In the evening the crowds staggered back again and Ovid closes with the delicate vignette of a tipsy old man supporting his tipsy old wife home. Unlike the *Salii*, Anna Perenna cannot be said to have had any religious meaning at all.

Even as a custom it was old-fashioned in Ovid's day and it seems to have died out soon after, as opportunities for leisure grew more sophisticated.

Unlike March, April was a busy month. Whatever its etymology, whether from an Etruscan word *Apru* or the Latin *aperio*—'the month when things open'—it wit-nessed a number of major ceremonies. Some of them had already by the early Empire degenerated into mere social observances—such as the quaint practice on 1 April when working-class women used to bathe in the public baths reserved for men and pray to Fortuna Virilis for good luck with men. For the rest of the year mixed bathing was strictly prohibited except for a short while under the later emperor Heliogabalus, who some-what perversely made it compulsory. So too the rich gave big parties on 4 April, on the occasion of the games in honour of Magna Mater, a Phrygian goddess, and the plebeians on 19 April, the festival of Ceres. Both customs must at one time have been connected closely with their respective religious festivals but the connexion had long since been forgotten. However, there were three festivals which did retain their significance for the citizens of Rome—the Parilia on 21 April, the Floralia on 28 April and the Feriae Latinae.

The Parilia was in honour of Pales, a pair of shep-herd-deities, whose origin was lost in such mists of antiquity that the great scholar Varro and others were uncertain whether Pales was singular or plural and, if the former, whether a god or goddess (p. 27). The pur-pose of the festival was to purify the sheep and the sheep-folds and to avert diseases from the flocks. In country districts it was still kept up in its original form, as Tibullus describes (II, 5, 81*ff.*) but unlike most of the other agricultural festivals it did not lose its popularity at Rome, because it was identified with the birthday of the city (which began on the Palatine Hill) and cele-brated as such. There was both an official public cere-mony, about which we know nothing, except that it was conducted by the *rex sacrorum*, and private celebrations of which Ovid gives an account. Rome was divided into thirty wards (*curiae*) and it is probable that each ward organised its own celebration. Houses were decorated with greenery and a large bonfire was built of bean-straw and laurel. When the fire was blazing well, the person in charge threw on to it a curious mixture of dried blood from a horse that had been sacrificed the preceding October (p. 96) and ashes of unborn calves, which had been torn from the wombs of pregnant cows sacrificed in each of the thirty wards a week earlier (the Fordicidia, on 15 April) and had been burnt. This macabre mixture, a purifying agent, was carefully stored by the Vestal Virgins who distributed a small ration of it for each bonfire on the Parilia. At the same time offerings of cakes and milk were made to Pales, but no blood sacrifice, and prayers were said. The climax came when the whole company, after sprinkling their hands with holy water from a laurel branch, jumped three times through the flames. The festival ended with a large open-air meal. The Parilia is interesting just because it managed to evolve from a purely pastoral festival into a national, and urban, one. Sheep were forgotten, but the rebirth and renewal of the city remained something for which people anxiously sought divine favour. Ovid himself—who was no zealot—says that he had taken part in jumping over the bonfire and two centuries later the day was still kept. Athenaeus' dinner-party guests were disturbed at their talk by the sound of pipes, drums, cymbals and singing as the citizens of Rome celebrated the Parilia.

Flora, the goddess who was responsible for the flowering of all things, was another deity that evolved with the times. Her cult was certainly very old, because she was one of the deities privileged to have a priest of her own, but some time towards the end of the third century a change came over her, which was no doubt a response to the emotional needs of the hour. In 238 B.C. the Sibylline Books were consulted because of a prolonged famine and recommended the institution of games in honour of Flora. These games, which by the time of Augustus lasted for a whole week from 28 April to 3 May, rapidly acquired their own character, which stressed the flowering not of plants and trees but of sex. This is clear from some odd details. The games themselves, held by the aediles in the Circus Maximus, were the normal combination of races, shows and fights but at their start, as Horace recalls (*Satires* II, 3, 182), the spectators were showered with vetches, beans and lupines—which they nibbled not so much to stave off hunger as to stimulate fertility. The same must be the point of unloosing wild hares and goats—notoriously highly sexed animals—on the last days of the games. But the distinctive feature was performance of strip-tease plays in the theatres. Valerius Maximus (II, 10, 8) tells the story of the younger Cato ostentatiously walking out from one, although he felt unwilling and unable actually to introduce legislation to prohibit them. Such incidents seem a far cry from modern piety, but they serve to remind us yet again that for the Romans the gods were to be found in the working of natural processes. Festivals, like the Floralia, can be found among many people and we should not be misled by the fierce disapproval of Christian fathers such as Lactantius and St. Augustine into supposing that Flora was not a real goddess for thousands of Romans.

By contrast the Feriae Latinae were a very serious affair. It was not strictly a Roman festival but a joint festival of the Romans and the Latins and it was celebrated not in Rome but on the principal summit of the Alban Hills, yet it occupied a dominant place in Roman life because the magistrates were expected to attend and only in exceptional circumstances were allowed to leave for their provinces before it. It dated back to very early times when Alba Longa rather than Rome was still the chief city of Latium, although so far no prehistoric remains have been found on the site of the temple of Jupiter Latiaris to whom the sacrifice was made. Originally all the neighbouring states (Pliny the Elder gives a list of some forty-seven names) sent their representatives, who made a common sacrifice of a white heifer which they then consumed in a communal meal. During the

time of the festival a truce prevailed throughout
Latium. By Cicero's day, however, many of these states
had disappeared from the map and were represented at
the festival by nominal delegates. For instance there was
no longer a community of Cabenses: instead a Roman
was nominated as 'the Cabensian priest' and acted for
the vanished people. And Rome had long ceased to be an
equal partner in the festival. She provided the organisa-
tion; it was her consuls who fixed its date—usually at
the end of April—every year when they entered office;
and the occasion itself became a symbol of Rome's world-
empire rather than of the community of Latin peoples.
Nevertheless it continued and much importance was
attached to it. The consuls went to it, accompanied by
a large retinue, and in their absence a prefect of the city
was appointed, although his function was so powerless
that under the Empire even children were sometimes
honoured with the office. But more significantly the
Romans respected its due celebration. It was a general
holiday, a time for catching up on one's correspondence
or going to pay visits to one's friend (Cicero, *On the
Republic* I, 14). Cicero refuses to announce a formal
engagement in the two days immediately following it
which were *religiosi* (*Letters to his brother Quintu*s 2,
4) and, if the festival had to be repeated because of some
slip in the procedure (see p. 35), even if the slip was an
imaginary one desired for political ends in order to
delay public business, the Romans accepted it without
question. It is not therefore surprising that the festival
was still elaborately conducted in the third century A.D.
It reflected the long memories of the Roman people
whose history taught that Rome's imperial greatness was
due in the first instance to the co-operation of the other
Latins and might therefore depend upon the divine per-
petuation of that co-operation.

'May' is another puzzling name, perhaps meaning
'growth' (cf. *maior* etc.) or else called after the obscure
and unimpressive goddess Maia, mother of Mercury,
but, although we think of it as a merry month, for the
Romans it was on the whole rather gloomy. It was un-

lucky, for instance, to be married in May. A number of the festivals which fall in the course of the month are also of a sinister character.

The chief was the Lemuria, the days of Ghosts, on 9, 11 and 13 May. Whereas the Parentalia had been concerned with the spirits of immediate relatives, the Lemuria was devoted to all the dead of the household who were thought of as coming to the surface and haunting the home on these days. The most potent spirits were those which had died young and therefore bore a grudge. One ancient scholar even defined *Lemures* as 'the wandering and terrifying shades of men who died before their time', but the word is more general and means 'ghosts' as a whole. What is certain is that the Romans took them seriously. The Lemuria were public festivals of long standing, but no record remains of what sacrifices were performed at them. All that does survive is Ovid's account of the ritual which every householder carried out privately. After rising at midnight and washing his hands, he walked barefoot through the house spitting nine black beans from his mouth. As he spat each bean, he looked away and intoned the magic spell 'with these I ransom me and mine'. The ghosts crept up and ate the beans, while with his back turned he washed his hands again and beat a loud gong. Then intoning another spell nine times ('ancestral ghosts, depart'), he looked round and the ghosts vanished. (It is a regular practice to avert one's eyes when sacrificing to or doing any business with powers of the underworld.)

At first sight it is difficult to imagine Livy or Horace or Agrippa solemnly getting out of bed and going through this ritual. And yet they probably did—at least in a modified form. One of the few surviving quotations of the easy-going Maecenas concerns the *Lemures* —'the irremediable faction on the look-out for food and drink haunts our dwellings and passes its death in hoping'—referring to the need of spirits for continual sustenance. This, as Heurgon has illustrated (*Daily Life of the Etruscans*, p. 267), ties in with the curious and widespread make-believe of constructing mosaics to resemble scrap-food (chicken bones, fish skeletons etc.), as a substitute for actually feeding the *Lemures*. So too Horace can, with every sign of conviction, evoke the picture of an innocent child returning to haunt the people who have cruelly murdered it (*Epodes* V, 92).

Roman religion was—even from the sixth century B.C.—an uneasy combination of Italian beliefs with Greek myths and, in considering the attitude of Augustan Romans to death, we are too apt to think first of the Greek myths of Styx, Acheron and the kingdom of Hades. This (despite its use by Virgil in *Aeneid* VI) was certainly not taken seriously by Virgil's contemporaries. Like Father Christmas, it was a fable believed only by old women (Cicero, *Tusculan Disputations* I, 48) and children (Juvenal, *Satires* II, 149*ff*.). 'Girls nowadays,' Propertius says (II, 34, 53–4), 'don't stop to ask whether anything remains of us after the Stygian waters.' This fact accounts for the surprising failure of Lucretius' great poem: it was tilting against a windmill, since his readers were not scared of the proverbial punishment of Hell, which he set out to ridicule. Some people were oppressed by a sense of nihilism, feeling that there was no existence after our present life—'We must sleep for one eternal night' (Catullus 5, 6) or, as Cicero sadly puts it, 'That long time, when I shall not exist, troubles me more than this brief life which yet seems to me too long' (*Letters to Atticus* XII, 18, 1). But most people, while rejecting the Greek vision of the after-life, cautiously accepted the hope or the fear that the spirit did in some sense survive. It is this belief which moved Tacitus to pray that the soul of Agricola may repose in peace 'if it be true that great souls are not extinguished with the body'. It is this belief, too, which inspired the deeply moving letter of consolation which Servius Sulpicius wrote to Cicero in 45 B.C. on the death of his daughter. Behind it lay the sanction of Stoicism that, when the soul has left the body, it subsists in the atmosphere until eventually it is dissolved into the great spirit of the universe. This is the faith which has left its mark on a thousand epitaphs.

So the *Lemuria* did still correspond to an anxiety which was felt deep down in the consciousness of most Romans, however much they might disown the Elysian fields or the tortures of Tartarus. Nothing shows this so clearly as the violent outburst of the elder Pliny (*Natural History* VIII, 190) who attacks 'the stupidity of those who renew life in death; where will creatures ever find rest if souls in heaven, if shades in hell, still have feeling?' Pliny's question could be answered: 'by celebrating the *Lemuria*'.

Human sacrifice—the most effective of all sacrifices—was never widely practised at Rome but, in moments of tension and hysteria, it did still happen, however much later Romans wished to cover up the fact. One of the last certain examples was the immolation of two Greeks and two Gauls after the battle of Cannae in 216 B.C. Its place was taken, under the civilising influence of the *pontifices*, by substitute sacrifices, one of which was held on 15 May. It was not an official state festival, although it was conducted by state-priests, since it was undertaken on behalf of the different quarters of the city and not of the city as a whole. Throughout Rome there were located twenty-seven small shrines, called *sacra Argeorum*, in which on 17 March there were deposited small rush-puppets, resembling men bound hand and foot. On 15 May a spectacular procession was held, in which the consuls or other magistrates, the *pontifices*, the Vestal Virgins and the Priestess of Jupiter, who put on mourning for this occasion in place of the wedding dress which she wore the rest of the time, went round collecting the puppets from the shrines and then dropped them into the river Tiber from the oldest bridge, the *Pons Sublicius.* Dionysius of Halicarnassus and Ovid had both witnessed the ceremony and been impressed by it. Its precise interpretation is disputed, but the most probable explanation is that the rush-puppets were a substitute for old men who used to be thrown into the river in times of acute famine as a human sacrifice. There is a record of such a sacrifice being performed in 440 B.C. and the custom had given rise to a proverb which was common in the time of Cicero—'off the bridge with the sixty-year-olds'.

In the days when Rome was still a farming community and not a busy commercial city, the chief anxiety of May was how the harvest would turn out. In Italy the corn ripens towards the end of the month and is usually cut at the beginning of June so that every precaution was taken to safeguard the crops at this critical stage. The accepted ritual—which still survives in Britain in the custom of beating the bounds during Ascension-tide in May—was to lead a procession of a bull, sheep and pig, three times round the fields and then to sacrifice them to Ceres, the goddess of growth, or Mars, the god of strength. This procession was called a lustration from *luere* (to loose) because it was believed that it freed the fields from harmful forces. The idea behind it is like that of a magic circle which is drawn round people or places and insulates them from external danger, just as the Romans used to protect their cities by driving a sacred furrow right round them (*pomerium*). Every farm and every village performed a lustration of its land during the course of the month and Virgil gives us a poetical account of such a ceremony in his *Georgics* (I, 388*ff*.): 'All the farm-hands should pray to Ceres and make her an offering of milk, honey and sweet wine. Then the victim should be led three times round the young crops, attended by the whole company singing and praying. No one should take the sickle to the ripe grain until he has crowned his head with a garland of oak and danced an impromptu dance of thanksgiving to Ceres.'

At Rome itself there were two ceremonies of this kind: the Amburbium, when the victims processed round the city to purify it, and the Ambarvalia, the procession round the fields. There is very little evidence about the Amburbium which had probably fallen into neglect by the end of the Republic, but it can be reconstructed by comparison with a similar ritual at the town of Gubbio, where the detailed procedure is preserved in an inscription. The Ambarvalia, however, did survive and are mentioned by the geographer Strabo who wrote under Augustus, but it is difficult to believe that, except in exceedingly primitive times, the Romans could have conducted a procession three times round the perimeter of their land in one day, for even if their territory only stretched five miles from the Forum, the total perimeter would have been over thirty-one miles and a bull cannot readily be persuaded to walk at more than two miles an hour. Strabo speaks of the priests at the Ambarvalia making sacrifices at certain fixed spots on the outskirts of the city, and this no doubt had replaced the original circular procession.

But although the Amburbium and the Ambarvalia no longer meant much to the average Roman, there was a related ritual, performed at irregular intervals, which did figure prominently in their lives. Every time the census was held and the register of Roman citizens with their financial circumstances was revised, the concluding ceremony was a lustration of the people of Rome, described by the phrase *lustrum condere*. The census had originally been designed to produce a list of people eligible for military service and the final lustration was, therefore, similar to the lustrations of armies which were normally held before important battles and campaigns. The people formed up in units outside the city boundary (usually in the Campus Martius) and the solemn procession of bull, sheep and pig was led three times round them before being sacrificed to Mars. Some idea of the impressive nature of the ceremony can be gained from a fine relief, depicting the scene, which is preserved in the Louvre Museum in Paris (see plate IV). The census, which should have been carried out every five years, had in fact lapsed since 70 B.C.—a casualty of the Civil Wars —but it was revived by Augustus, who recalls in his *Res Gestae* that he held the census and performed the *lustrum* three times during his reign, in 28 B.C., 8 B.C. and A.D. 14. Casual references in contemporary writers make it clear that whenever the lustration at the end of the census was held under the early Empire, it was attended by a large and curious crowd.

Like May, the first part of June was regarded as inauspicious. Ovid pretends to have consulted the wife of the *flamen Dialis* about his daughter's marriage and to have been advised to wait until after 15 June. Several of the days, perhaps the whole of the week 7–15 June, were defined as *religiosi*, on which no public or private business was done, journeys were avoided and, wherever possible, military activities suspended. The reason for this is not clear, but the central event of the period was one which had been crucial in the life of early Rome and which retained strong sentimental interest down to the very end of the Roman Empire.

The shrine of Vesta was the symbolic hearth of Rome. It represented all the essential elements of the domestic life of the Roman family. Here, in a small round temple in the Forum, was the holy fire which was rekindled every 1 March by rubbing two sticks together and was looked after for the rest of the year by the Vestal Virgins. Here was the store-house (*penus*) where were kept not only the sacred elements used in various rituals throughout the year, such as the ashes for the Parilia (p. 82), but also certain precious objects, such as a statue of Athena said to have been rescued from Troy, which guaranteed the lasting prosperity of Rome, and two small statuettes representing the Penates (gods of the *penus* or storehouse) of the Roman People, who were respected as guardian deities of the state. When the Romans once thought of founding a new capital city on a different site, Livy makes Camillus plead eloquently against the plan, by appealing to 'the undying fires of Vesta and the statue which is kept in Vesta's temple as a guarantee of success. Are we to allow all these relics which are as old or older than the foundation of Rome itself to be abandoned and profaned?' (Livy V, 52, 7). The cult of Vesta was symbolic of the eternal power of Rome. Her treasures were jealously guarded: the store-house was kept shut throughout the rest of the year and only the Vestals and the *pontifex maximus* were allowed to enter it. But on

9 June each year it was opened to married women who processed to it with bare feet and brought simple food-offerings with them. It was an impressive sight, which made Ovid stop and gaze, just as a tourist today will pause to watch the penitents climbing the Scala Santa on their knees. By Ovid's time the festival of the Vestalia was also celebrated as the bakers' holiday, because the Vestals were responsible for making by hand a special salted flour (*mola salsa*) which was used in several rituals and which was no doubt a survival from primitive times when each family made its own bread. A pretty fresco from Pompeii shows a miller's donkey decorated with garlands and little cakes in honour of the day.

We do not know what happened during the rest of the week, but on 15 June the Vestals swept out their store-house and carried all the rubbish from it to the river Tiber. Once the shrine had been cleaned in this way, the unlucky period was over and life could return to normal. Hence the day was distinguished with the peculiar letters Q.ST.D.F. in the calendars, which meant that the day was a working day as soon as the rubbish had been cleared away (*Quando Stercus Delatum Fas*). But Roman religion is full of surprises. It might be expected that this solemn week would be marked, like Holy Week by quiet and sober behaviour, but in fact the Ides of June (the 13th) were one of the rowdiest nights of the year. The guild of flute-players who, as we have seen (p. 44), were indispensable at sacrifices, held a drunken dinner that evening in the temple of Minerva on the Aventine, at the end of which, masked and dressed in long robes, they roamed the streets of the city. Sensible citizens locked their doors and stayed at home on that night.

The other great festival of June was the festival of Fors Fortuna on the far bank of the Tiber on 24 June. There were at least two shrines of Fortuna a mile or so downstream from Rome, one of which was traditionally said to have been founded by the sixth king of Rome, Servius Tullius. Perhaps because luck is no respecter of persons or classes, Fortune was always a popular goddess

with the poorer elements at Rome. Indeed this was one
of the very few cults which slaves could attend as well as
free persons. Normally a slave or a prisoner was thought
to pollute any religious ceremony at which he happened
to be present, so that elaborate precautions were taken
to exclude them before the proceedings began. We find
a notice fixed to a statue of Mars 'His statue is not to
be touched by a slave'. Even women were forbidden
to attend sacrifices to Mars and Hercules—Hercules
because, as Propertius says (IV, 9, 70), they once refused
him a drink of water when he was thirsty. But all could
share in the worship of Fortune and on 24 June crowds
poured out of Rome, on foot and by boat, to witness the
sacrifices at the shrines of Fortune. The scene on the
river was particularly gay, as Cicero (*de Finibus* V, 70)
and Ovid (*Fasti* VI, 775*ff*.) describe it, with flotillas of
little boats racing one another down the swift-flowing
current. The banks were packed with happy picnickers,
who, Ovid says, were not ashamed to come home drunk.
Like the festival of Anna Perenna on 15 March it was a
great popular holiday, but, as a series of dedications
show, it was also a genuinely religious occasion.

By contrast July's festivals were utterly obscure. Such
occasions as the Lucaria (on 19 and 21 July) and the Fur-
rinalia (on 25 July) were in classical times only celebrated by professional priests connected with the cults and
did not impinge at all upon the religious consciousness
of the people in general. The one event which did command popular support, the Games of Apollo, held from
the 6th to the 13th of the month, had by the end of the
Republic almost entirely lost their religious character.
Plays were performed and gladiatorial combats staged,
but the connexion with the worship of the god was very
remote. When Atticus took his daughter to watch the
games of Victory in 45 B.C., Cicero approved but his comment is revealing: 'It is indeed something for one's mind
to relax both at the spectacle and at the impression of
religious feeling' (*Letters to Atticus* XIII, 44, 2).

With August we return to popular and well-patron-
ised festivals. The most notable of them was held on 12

August when the praetor sacrificed a heifer to Hercules at a very old round temple near the entrance to the Circus Maximus. Hercules was a Greek import, who had long been naturalised at Rome and whose worship was looked after by a special body of public slaves. In the course of a long and varied life on earth Hercules had brought off a series of remarkable coups, many of them shady and most of them unscrupulous. This trait endeared him to Roman businessmen who looked to him for help and inspiration and who rewarded his services by offering a tithe of their profits on his altar (the *ara maxima*) on this day. The millionaire Crassus on one occasion dedicated a tenth of his entire fortune, but his object seems to have been chiefly to show Romans just how wealthy he was. More typical are the hoards of small inscriptions recording dedications by traders and others and the passing references to the custom in comic poets. Early in the first century B.C. L. Munius, who admittedly described himself as 'old-fashioned', set up a small inscription to Hercules Victor at Reate, a Sabine town some fifty miles from Rome. On it he records that he offers a tenth of his profits to the god but asks that the god will help him with his accounts to make sure that he has got the sum right! It is not clear what happened to all these tithes. The upkeep of Hercules' cult cannot have been an expensive business and there is no record that his temples contained vast treasures. It seems probable that the money was used to provide a free meal for anyone who wanted it on the day of the festival. For there was a long-standing prohibition against any part of the sacrificed animal being removed from Hercules' precinct, which must have meant that it was eaten on the spot and the remains burned. This would soon have developed into a public feast.

The following day (13 August) was the anniversary of Diana on the Aventine. Originally the cult of Diana had been closely linked with politics. It was founded by king Servius Tullius as a means of uniting the Latin peoples with Rome, on the model of some of the great federal cults of Greece, such as the Ionian sanctuary of Artemis at Ephesus. This function was forgotten once the Romans and the Latins were fused into one nation, although the original regulations of the cult, written in Greek letters, survived down to the time of Augustus and were deciphered by the historian Dionysius. Instead, the temple became the focus for slaves (perhaps helped by a bogus connexion between the Latin word *servus*, a slave, and 'Servius'). It was one of the few cults which slaves could attend without polluting the proceedings and her festival was kept as a summer holiday for slaves, corresponding to the winter Saturnalia (p. 98). Every Roman had to give his slaves the day off. But why Roman women should choose this particular day to wash their hair is not at all clear.

Diana is a good example of a deity whose role had changed completely during the five centuries of the Republic but who still remained powerful and revered. Another was Consus. His name means 'storer' (cf. *condere*) and he was the god of the granary, worshipped in an underground barn in the Circus Maximus. The site of Consus' shrine lay in the middle of the city's most frequented race-course and his festival, on 21 August, was by tradition connected with a popular legend, the Rape of the Sabine Women, because the Sabines were so engrossed in watching the games held in honour of Consus that the Romans were able to steal their women unopposed. So Consus was thought of more in terms of horse-racing—a sport to which the Romans were passionately addicted, although Ovid advised one to go to watch the pretty girls, not the horses—rather than of corn-storage. Dionysius says that sacrifice was still made at his shrine before the races and we know that on this day it was the custom to garland horses and mules with flowers in his honour. The Circus Maximus held thousands of people and it must have been a solemn moment as a hush fell on the great crowd while the priest of Quirinus and the Vestal Virgins went in procession to perform the sacrifices at the start of the day's programme. Today Cup Final crowds sing 'Abide with Me'.

September resembles July in that it made up for a

lack of important festivals by a fortnight of games—the Ludi Romani, which ran from the 5th to the 19th of September in the late Republic. But if the games themselves were conspicuously irreligious, there were two events connected with them which were prominent in the religious life of the city. The 13th of September was the day on which the temple of Jupiter Optimus Maximus, the patron god of Rome, had been dedicated in the year 507 B.C. Although the temple itself had been rebuilt and enlarged several times, it retained its position as the religious centre of Rome. For centuries a nail had been driven annually into the walls of the temple as a protection against plague; sight-seers in Sulla's day could still see and count the rows of rusty nails. But if that ceremony seems to have lapsed by the first century B.C., it had been replaced by a much more magnificent one. As a sequel to the appropriate sacrifice of a white heifer to Jupiter by the consul on this day, the whole body of senators and magistrates met at the temple and sat down to a banquet. But it was more than the usual meal at which the remains of the sacrificed animal were eaten, for special couches and chairs were set out on which the statues of Jupiter, Juno and Minerva, dressed in fine robes and impressively made up, were placed so that they too could share with human beings in the good things of the table.

A similar banquet was held on the Ides of November in the middle of the plebeian games and both were occasions which brought senators hurrying back to Rome. At such times, Seneca said, the gods seem very real and very close. The other great event, which was also enacted in the plebeian games in November, was the procession from the Capitol through the Forum to the Circus, that is right through the busiest part of the city. We have two eye-witness accounts of this procession, one by Dionysius (*Roman Antiquities* VII, 70ff.), and the other by Ovid (*Loves* III, 2, 43ff.) in an amusing description of the attractions and discomforts of a day at the games. Young boys on foot and on horseback led the way. Then came the competitors, charioteers driving their teams of horses, athletes stripped for action and, presumably, gladiators ready for battle. Behind them were groups of dancers, boys and men, dressed in scarlet tunics and armed with swords and short spears, who jigged their way through the streets to the sound of pipes. Then came clowns, miming and joking with the crowds that lined the way. As the heart of the procession was reached, massed bands of pipes and harps and clouds of incense rising from the thuribles of a hundred incense-bearers heralded the approach of the carriages in which the statues and emblems of the gods were borne. When the procession reached the Circus, the statues were care-fully placed on special couches, which Augustus took credit for restoring (*Res Gestae* XIX, 1), where they could watch the games in comfort. Despite the fondness and talent of the people of Italy for processions of this kind, it is unlikely that the *pompa circensis,* as it was called, took place on each day of the games. It is more probable that it was organised on the most important day, perhaps 15 September.

Horse-racing again provided the main religious event of October but now there were more sinister overtones. October was the month when the farmer cleaned his tools and the soldier his weapons and put them away until they were needed again the following spring. Hence in the old religious calendar there is a resem-blance between the festivals of March and those of October. The Purification of Arms on 19 October cor-responds to a similar purification on 19 March but by the late Republic both had become purely formal and antiquarian rituals. The only ceremony which main-tained its popularity was a macabre affair on 15 October. Chariot-races, again corresponding to a parallel festival of horse-races on 14 March, were held on this day in the Campus Martius. The near-side horse of the winning pair in the most important race was sacrificed to Mars. Its tail was cut off and rushed to the *regia* so that the blood might drip on to the ashes of the sacred hearth which were subsequently used as an ingredient at the Parilia (p. 82). The horse's head was also cut off and

probably stuck on the outside of the *regia*. In earlier
times it had been fought for by the inhabitants of two of
the chief parishes of Rome, the Via Sacra and the
Subura, but this practice had died out before the first
century B.C. and the significant action of Julius Caesar
in October 46 B.C. who sacrificed two mutinous soldiers
and nailed their heads on the outside of the *regia* suggests that this was what happened to the October horse's
head too. In any event the tradition went on and the
people of Rome retained a superstitious interest in it.

November was the third of the blank months, relieved
only by the fortnight of the plebeian games (4–17
November) and a feast of Jupiter (*epulum Jovis*) on the
Ides (see above, p. 72). December, however, was very
busy. Early in the month the leading women of Rome,
including the Vestal Virgins, celebrated a movable
festival of the 'good goddess', Bona Dea, by night in the
house of a magistrate. In 63 B.C. it had been held in
Cicero's house, in 62 B.C. in Caesar's (perhaps in the
regia, since that was his official residence as *pontifex
maximus*). The latter occasion gave rise to a notorious
scandal. The cult was evidently designed to promote the
fertility of women—a pig was the victim—and all men
were rigorously excluded. A young aristocrat, however,
called P. Clodius dressed himself up as a woman and
tried to attend. Unfortunately he was detected and, as a
result, mercilessly mocked by Cicero which led to a
bitter feud between the two men in which Clodius got
his revenge by engineering the exile of Cicero in 58 B.C.
Clodius' motive for this escapade is uncertain: gossip
made out that he was having an affair with Caesar's wife
but it is more probable that it was just a high-spirited
prank. In any event the righteous indignation which
Cicero was able to stir up in his speeches on the subject
shows how seriously the goddess was respected at large.
The festival itself had to be held afresh on another
night, because it had been desecrated by the presence of
a man (cf. p. 35 *instauratio*). Bona Dea was a popular
goddess throughout Italy under the Empire. She had at
least two temples at Ostia and numerous inscriptions

attest her worship in Rome and the provinces. We should, therefore, not take too seriously the vicious attacks by Juvenal (II, 83*ff*.; VI, 314*ff*.) who makes out that her worship was kept up only by drunken perverts. This is pure rhetoric—the stuff of ancient satire—and Juvenal, after all, as a man, can hardly have known what actually went on. The evidence points rather to it as a decorous and deeply felt cult.

The year ended, as the modern year ends, with a great holiday of peace and good will. Indeed the customs of Christians are directly derived from the ancient festival of the Saturnalia, originally confined to 17 December but later extending over several days. Saturn, who began as a blight-god, at an early stage was assimilated to the Greek Cronus, the father of Zeus, and so came to stand for the good old days, the Golden Age which had formerly existed but which might be renewed once again. It is in this spirit that Virgil speaks in *Eclogue* 4 of the return of the kingdom of Saturn—*redeunt Saturnia regna*. The holiday was opened by a great sacrifice at the temple of Saturn in the Forum, followed by a public banquet which anyone could attend. Shops were shut, schools were closed, law-courts deserted: the whole city was *en fête*. Everyone discarded the formal toga and dressed instead in loose holiday clothes (*synthesis*) and wore soft caps (*pileus*) on their heads, recalling the paper hats which we wear after Christmas dinner. The streets were thronged with strolling crowds, who on this one occasion of the year were allowed to play gambling games in public. Martial tells in a poem (14, 1) how at the Saturnalia people could throw dice openly without fear of the police. Within the family the festivities were relaxed and gay. Slaves were given all the privileges of freedom and were waited on at meals by their masters. Each house chose a mock king as Master of the Revels— a tradition that lasted down to recent times at Twelfth Night; Tacitus tells how Nero abused his position as 'King' to humiliate the young prince Britannicus (*Annals* XII, 15). Parents gave toys to their children, particularly little earthenware dolls (*sigilla*); friends exchanged candles (*cerei*); families went 'first-footing' to each other's homes.

It is a pleasant note on which to leave the yearly round of religious festivals. Some Romans were patronisingly superior about it, like Seneca who argued that one should observe the Saturnalia but should observe it by frugal contemplation and not with idle enjoyment, or the younger Pliny who built himself a sound-proof room to which he retired for the duration of the holiday (*Letters* II, 17, 24), but others appreciated the simple significance of it. Men were united to men in good will by the god. Here was living proof of how the gods could be conciliated so as to co-operate and make things go well for mankind. There is no finer statement of this than a little poem by Statius (*Silvae* I, 6) written under the emperor Domitian. He emphasises how the Saturnalia make all men equal:

> Rich or poor, whoever he is, he boasts that he shares the table of the emperor,

and how it brings happiness to the whole people:

> Time shall not fade that sacred day, so long as the hills of Latium stand, so long, father Tiber, as your city of Rome shall stand and the Capitol remain on earth.

6

Private Religion

MOST of the ceremonies discussed in the previous chapter were performed by special individuals on behalf of the state as a whole. What mattered was that they should be performed in the right way at the right time; the attendance of the Roman people as a whole at them was not necessary for their success, although, as a matter of fact, many of them drew large crowds of interested and devout spectators. Within the state there were smaller units—clubs, tribes, regiments, guilds, parishes and so on—each of which had its own patron gods and its own religious rites designed to ensure the continued prosperity of the group. Thus every clan (*gens*) seems to have had certain particular cults of its own. The Fabii had a shrine on the Quirinal Hill which they dared to maintain even when Rome was occupied by the Gauls; the Aurelii worshipped the Sun (*Sol*) as their distinctive god. Each legion of the Roman army had its protecting deity to whom prayer was offered and sacrifice made. The various guilds of traders at Ostia had their own chapels for the worship of the different gods who watched over their interests.

The smallest group within the community was the family. The family needs divine co-operation for the success of its day-to-day life just as much as the state, and the head of the family was responsible for taking the proper steps to secure that co-operation. Normally, as in public religion, this was a matter of carrying out certain regularly recurring ceremonies, but there could always arise sudden crises which called for special measures. The action to be taken in such a crisis would depend on the circumstances, but usually the person concerned would make a vow to the appropriate god (p. 25). Most Romans felt a special regard for a particular god whom they would ask to help in times of trouble. Just as Sulla always carried with him an image of Apollo, so, two hundred and fifty years later, Apuleius wrote that it was his habit to pack an image of his patron deity with his books and take it with him wherever he went (*Apology* 63) so that he could offer incense, wine and sometimes a sacrificial victim to it on solemn occasions. Personal religion for the Romans was primarily belief in the protection given by a particular god. Few Romans would take any important decision in their private affairs without first ascertaining the will of the god by some means of divination (p. 63).

In addition, however, to such well-known and identifiable gods, every Roman family also worshipped two separate groups of divine powers who controlled its destinies—the Lares and Penates. The Lares were the deified spirits of dead ancestors, who still took an interest in the family and were capable, if roused, of violent emotion. An old inscription has been discovered recently by the river Numicus near Rome, set up to Lar Aeneas, that is, Aeneas as the deified ancestor of all the Romans. The Romans referred to such spirits collectively as the *Di Indigites*. Virgil, for instance, prays to the *Di Indigites* of Rome, Romulus and Vesta—as the powers most intimately concerned with the fortunes of the city of Rome—to co-operate with Octavian in his attempts to restore peace to Italy after the Civil Wars (*Georgics* I, 498). But within the family they were known simply as the Lares and every household had its *Lararium* or shrine where offerings could be made to them. This shrine was like a cupboard, containing small statuettes representing the Lares, and stood in a corner of the main room of the house. It was the first thing to catch Encolpius' eye when he entered Trimalchio's house (Petronius, *Satyricon* 29). It was also often used as a kind of reliquary where other objects of value could be kept. Trimalchio, for instance, preserved the shavings of his first beard in a golden box there. Members of the family used to pray to their Lares every day and, perhaps, offer them some small gift, such as incense or wine (Plautus, *Aulularia* Prologue).

The other class of household gods were the Penates—
the powers that watched over the larder or store-house.
Just as the Roman people as a whole had their symbolic
hearth (Vesta) and Penates (p. 90), so each constituent
family honoured the spirits that ensured that they had
enough food to eat each day. Roman families offered
prayers to Vesta before the main meal of the day and in
the morning, on festivals, placed a garland of flowers
beside the hearth (Cato, *On agriculture* 142). More
devout households in the middle of their meal would
throw a small piece of cake on to the fire, as an offering
to Vesta. It was a good sign if it crackled as it burnt.
Such acts were probably not much observed by the late
Republic, for it would seem, from Horace, that they
were regarded as simple-minded superstitions in his
time. In a gently ironic ode (III, 23) he urges an imaginary country girl to propitiate the 'little gods' (the Lares)
with incense, fresh corn and a sucking-pig, to garland
them with rosemary and myrtle and to approach with
clean hands the altar of the Penates. The point of the
poem is not immediately obvious. In a sense it embodies
the principle that the gods respect simple offerings from
humble people as much as rich and extravagant gifts,
but this is to make it too much of a sermon and too little
of a poem. The wit lies rather in the expression of un-
sophisticated country superstitions in highly sophisticated language. Nevertheless, even if men like Cicero
or Caesar did not always 'say grace before dinner', the
Lares and Penates meant as much emotionally to them
as 'home' does to us.

All the important stages of life in the family were
carefully observed. Childbirth, in particular, was a
dangerous and chancy business where the co-operation
of Juno Lucina was essential. As soon as a baby was born,
evil spirits were elaborately expelled from the house
(p. 13) and the child was laid on the ground until its
father lifted it up with a ritual gesture. It was considered
ominous that Nero was touched by the rays of the sun
before he had felt the earth (Suetonius, *Nero* VI). If the
baby was a girl, a couch was spread for Juno in the

house; if it was a boy, a table was laid for Hercules. This thank-offering to the deity who had assisted at the birth remained for eight or nine days until the child and its mother were purified and the child was named. These were critical days when divine protection was particularly needed.

Puberty was a further significant stage. At the age of fourteen or so a boy dedicated the amulet (*bulla*) which he had worn as a charm during his childhood. In the presence of his family and friends he put off the striped toga and put on for the first time the plain toga of manhood. He was escorted to the Forum and introduced to public life. His name was officially enrolled on the list of citizens. But it was the religious aspect of the occasion that was at least as significant. Sacrifices were made for the boy's safe arrival at manhood. The Liberalia (17 March) was the festival originally reserved for this ceremony, but other days were also used. We know, for instance, that Virgil assumed the *toga virilis* on 15 October and Nero on 7 July. Even the most sceptical Romans kept up the ceremony and regarded it as their duty to attend the coming-of-age of their friends' children. Pliny the Younger counted it a regular item of his busy round of engagements when in Rome (*Letters* I, 9, 2).

Although there was no necessity at Rome for a marriage to be performed either by religious or by civil authorities, as it is, for instance, in Britain, the usual practice was for a wedding in fact to be celebrated with religious rites. A marriage was perfectly valid if the two parties were eligible (i.e. free citizens, of age, and legally independent) and merely consented to be married. Thus by Roman standards the casual union of Dido and Aeneas was in itself a legal marriage. Marriage is, however, an event of such magnitude that the co-operation of the gods is essential to its success and the Romans evolved an elaborate ritual in which the divine will was ascertained by divination and divine assistance sought by sacrifice. Then followed the wedding itself which culminated in the procession which transported the bride to her husband's house. Associated with the procession was a variety of superstitious customs, such as the throwing of nuts and the shouting of dirty jokes, which can best be appreciated from reading Catullus' wedding-hymns (61, 62), although he has to some extent mixed Greek and Roman elements. Each incident, however, had a specific religious purpose. One custom, which still survives today, was for the bridegroom to carry his bride over the threshold. He did this in case she should stumble which would be very unlucky: for the bride's entry to her new home would indicate how her future married life would go. So every precaution was taken to ensure that all went well. The door-posts themselves were decorated with wool and anointed as a means of conciliating the spirits which operated them.

The last great human drama is death. When all the appeals to the gods of healing, Apollo, Aesculapius and the rest, had proved unavailing, there only remained the task of dealing piously with the dead. In Augustan as in late Republican times, cremation was the almost universal method of disposing of a body. The practice of burial had, for whatever reason, been discontinued by the second century or earlier and was not revived until the age of Hadrian. Because the powers of the underworld are by their very nature sinister, great care was taken over funerals. The body, washed, anointed and dressed in fine clothes, was carried in procession either to a public crematorium (*ustrina*) or to the private burial ground where a corner of the land was reserved for lighting the funeral pyre. A relative, with his face averted as always when in the vicinity of gods, put a torch to the pyre. When the fire had died down, the ashes were gathered in an urn and deposited in the family vault, together with such necessities as the soul might need after death. The home, meanwhile, was in mourning until, after eight days, a sacrifice had been made to the Lares, which the deceased had now in a sense joined, and a ritual purification of the building had been carried out. These acts did not, however, end the duty of the living to the dead. As we have seen, the cult of the dead was one of the most persistent survivals at Rome (p. 75).

In the main private worship was a miniature of public worship, but it remained in many ways more naive and less developed. Magic and superstition were always very close to the surface of the ceremonies which the householder performed. The reason for this lies partly in the very fact that it was private. It was not subject in the same way to the civilising influence which generations of highly intelligent *pontifices* and statesmen had had on the procedures for public worship. Spells and incantations, for instance, played no part in official religious ceremonies and as early as 450 B.C. the legislators of the Twelve Tables had attempted to eradicate them from private life as well. But, in fact, they continued throughout the classical period as one of the most common phenomena of everyday life. Some were innocuous enough, like the spell which Caesar repeated three times to himself every time he took his seat in a carriage as an insurance against accidents (Pliny, *Natural History* XXVIII, 19). Some are pathetic and desperate attempts to cure or ward off disease. Others, however, reveal hidden forces of crude malevolence, such as the curses (*defixiones*) inscribed on lead which have been found in large numbers all over the Roman Empire. It is also true that, as Rome grew from a farming community into a city, the ordinary citizen lost much of his importance and individuality and became more and more one of a crowd. His prosperity depended less on his own efforts, and hence on his own success in securing the collaboration of the gods, and more on the favour of the state as a whole and of the leading men. It is therefore not surprising that, except for social occasions such as weddings, we hear comparatively little about the ritual of the family or household in the chief classical authors. It did not mean as much to them and their readers as the religion of the community of which they were part.

7
The Priests

THE complicated procedure of Roman religion required competent and authoritative supervision, but the Romans are almost unique in not having a separate priestly profession. With the exception of the *rex sacrorum* and the *flamen Dialis* (for which see below) the major offices of religion were usually held by prominent figures of political life. Cicero justifies this state of affairs by saying that as a result the 'most distinguished citizens safeguard religion by the good administration of the state and safeguard the state by the wise conduct of religion' (*On his house* 1). In fact it was a natural consequence of a religion which saw the clearest evidence of divine activity in the ordinary operations of human life. A priesthood came to be thought of both as an important social distinction and also as a useful lever in politics. Cicero was proud to be elected an augur, despite his scepticism on augury as a science. The place of priesthoods at Rome thus ensured that religion could never be wholly neglected. Anyone who aimed at a public career had also to take account of religion.

In the late Republic and early Empire there were four chief colleges of priests which were generally responsible for the maintenance of the cult of the gods. There were sixteen *pontifices*, sixteen augurs, fifteen men designated *sacris faciendis* ('for conducting sacrifices') and ten *epulones*. The members inside each college were of equal status but the augurs and *pontifices* were reckoned as rather more distinguished than the other two colleges. All the priesthoods, unlike a political magistracy, could be held for life. Since there were only some sixty priesthoods of major rite to be shared among 200–400 ambitious public figures competing for them at any one time, it was virtually unheard of for anyone to hold more than one during his life-time. Julius Caesar was *pontifex maximus* and augur. Only the emperor would be a member of all the colleges, as, for instance, Augustus records in his *Res Gestae* (VII, 3). It also meant that there might be a long delay before one gained a priesthood. Cicero, who had been consul in 63 B.C., did not become augur until ten years later. Pliny the Younger congratulates himself that he had done better than Cicero (*Letters* IV, 8, 5): he was consul in A.D. 100 and elected augur in A.D. 103. It is a disturbing clue to the close nature of Tacitus' relations with Domitian that he became a *quindecimvir sacris faciendis* in A.D. 88 nearly ten years *before* he was consul.

In early times the members of the four great colleges had been co-opted, but this method of selection tended to perpetuate a very closed circle of membership. In 103 B.C. a more complicated system was instituted as a result of popular pressure. The existing members put forward a series of nominations for any vacant place. The final choice was made by an *ad hoc* assembly of seventeen out of the thirty-five tribes. The successful candidate was then admitted to membership after proper ceremonies for ensuring the concurrence of the gods. Under the Empire the same system of nomination was used, except that the emperor had a special right to 'commend' a particular candidate (whose election was thereby assured), and the actual election was conducted by the Senate instead of the tribes.

The senior college was undoubtedly that of the *pontifices*. Originally, as their name 'bridge-builders' suggests, charged with the sacred duties involved in the construction and maintenance of bridges, they had, shortly after the expulsion of the kings, annexed the overall responsibility for the conduct of religion at Rome and were recognised as the premier priesthood. Successive colleges had compiled over the years a manual of religious precedents, the *Commentaries of the Pontifices*, which they invoked for determining all disputed questions of procedure. They advised what to do if a sacrifice went wrong or a sinister prodigy was reported. They had ultimate authority over the religious calendar,

fixing holy days, deciding when to insert an intercalary
month, and so on. At their head was the *pontifex
maximus*, who was elected as such and not chosen from
among the existing *pontifices*. Although expected to consult the rest of the college, he had a great deal of power
and freedom of action. His official residence was the
Palace (*regia*) in the centre of the Forum, where the
pontifical archives were kept. He also seems to have had
a general jurisdiction over all the other priests, including
the Vestal Virgins. Cicero quotes an instance from the
second century when the *pontifex maximus* of the day
fined the priest of Quirinus, who happened to be consul
at the time (*Philippics* XI, 18). It was by virtue of this
office that Julius Caesar was able to institute several
notable reforms, above all the reform of the calendar
which has lasted practically unchanged down to modern
times.

In addition to the sixteen *pontifices*, the pontifical
college also included for all practical purposes three
other bodies—the Vestals, the *flamines* and the *rex
sacrorum*. The Vestals, six in number, were chosen, presumably by the *pontifex maximus*, as young girls from
the old patrician families of Rome. They served for
thirty years as the guardians of the sacred and undying
fire of Vesta. They had other complicated rituals to perform such as the drawing of holy water and the preparation of the special salted meal (*mola salsa*) used in
certain sacrifices. They were also responsible for the
precious objects stored in the treasury of the temple of
Vesta. It was a great honour to be a Vestal and there
seems to have been no difficulty in getting recruits,
even though they were not allowed to marry until they
had completed their thirty years' service and any mis-
demeanour was very severely punished. A Vestal found
guilty of inchastity was buried alive.

The *flamines* were the priests of certain named gods.
There were twelve minor *flamines* (e.g. of Flora,
Pomona, Furrina) and three major *flamines*—of Jupiter,
Mars and Quirinus. Because each of them was concerned
with a particular god and a particular cult, these priest-

hoods were very much more professional and technical than the *pontifices*. Consequently, although nothing prevented them from being held jointly with political office, in fact they were not usually sought after by men engaged in active politics. They were rather the province of pious antiquarians, like the *flamen* of Quirinus whom Ovid met one day on a walk. Their job was to see that the cult and temple of their respective gods was kept up. Indeed the *flamen Dialis*, as the *flamen* of Jupiter was called, was so hedged about by restrictions and taboos of various kinds that it would have been difficult for him to have led an ordinary public life. One *flamen Dialis* did indeed become aedile in 200 B.C., but when a vacancy occurred in 87 B.C. the office was so uninviting that it could not be filled and it remained empty for seventy-five years until Augustus' efforts produced a candidate. Aulus Gellius, a scholar writing in the second century A.D., has prescribed a fascinating list of these restrictions which include the following (*Attic Nights* X, 15): the *flamen Dialis* was not allowed to ride a horse, to spend more than one night outside the city, to touch goats, uncooked meat, ivy or beans, to have his hair cut except by a free citizen, to look upon an army, to swear an oath. All of these correspond to intelligible, if primitive, superstitions but they did not conspire to make his life any easier.

The very obscurity of many of the deities which had *flamines* as well as the curious position of the *flamen Dialis* indicate that these priesthoods were relics from the very earliest days of Rome. So too was the third supernumerary in the pontifical college—the *rex sacrorum* or King of Ceremonies. During the monarchy the Roman kings had enjoyed temporal and spiritual power. When they were expelled, the Republican magistracy took over most of their temporal powers and some of their religious rights and duties. What was left was assigned to a substitute king, the *rex sacrorum*; who, nominally at least, took precedence in all religious ceremonies. In practice, however, his functions were entirely usurped by the *pontifices* and by the late Republic the office was of no significance. Cicero and his contemporaries hardly ever refer to it and the survival of the office is best seen in early imperial sculptures which show gatherings of the leading priests at sacrifices or other ceremonies.

Little need be said about the college of augurs whose functions have been outlined in the chapter on divination (p. 55). Just as a corpus of pontifical law had been evolved over the centuries, so too there was a standard collection of precedents for the interpretation of omens to which the augurs could refer. The *quindecimviri sacris faciendis* were chiefly responsible for guarding and, on occasion, consulting the Sibylline Books (p. 62). This, however, was a very infrequent occurrence and for the rest of their time they exercised a general supervision over all cults of a foreign rather than Latin origin. For example, it was the *quindecimviri* who were responsible, as Lucan says (I, 599ff.), for washing on every 27 March the black stone which represented the Phrygian goddess, Magna Mater, Cybele. The cult of the goddess had been introduced to Rome in a crisis of the Punic Wars on the recommendation of the Sibylline Books, but for two centuries it was treated with distant reserve: apart from the *quindecimviri,* no other Roman was allowed to take part in the cult.

As public banquets became an increasingly common feature of the great festivals and games, so the need arose for a special body of men to see that all the arrangements went smoothly. The college of *epulones* ('feast-organisers') was founded in 196 B.C. and its membership had grown to ten by the time of Caesar, which is some indication of the prominence of such feasts in the life of the city. They were chiefly concerned with the dinners of the Senate following sacrifices on the festivals of Jupiter Optimus Maximus and with the public banquets at the Roman and Plebeian Games. They doubtless left the detailed administration of these arrangements to underlings, probably public slaves.

These then were the four major priesthoods which

shared between them the overall supervision of Roman religion. In addition there were numerous particular bodies concerned with different rituals, such as the *Salii* (p. 79), the *Luperci* (p. 77) and the Arval Brethren (p. 39).

8

Religion in the Time of Augustus

AFTER the battle of Actium in 31 B.C. the predominant emotions in Roman minds seem to have been guilt and relief. As they looked back on the history of the last fifty years, the one clear mistake which all could see was that they had omitted to carry out their religious observances dutifully. Priesthoods, like the *flamen Dialis*, had been left unfilled; temples, like that of Jupiter Feretrius on the Capitol which Atticus had visited about 33 B.C. (Nepos, *Atticus* XX, 3), had fallen into disrepair; ceremonies had been omitted or neglected; divination had been made a mockery by the activities of men like Bibulus (p. 58) in 59 B.C. Here was a rational and comforting explanation of why things had gone so wrong. Four hundred years later, in A.D. 384, exactly the same arguments could be used. The great pagan orator, Symmachus, pleaded for the restoration of the Altar of Victory by claiming that when religion is affronted the whole state suffers and disasters ensue. It was the maintenance of ancestral rites that subdued the world to Roman arms and drove the Gauls and Hannibal from the walls.

The same ideas are found spontaneously in many writers during the reign of Augustus. None puts it better than Horace when he writes (*Odes* III, 6, 1): 'You will pay for the sins of your ancestors, Romans, until you repair the ruined temples of the gods, and the images begrimed with smoke.' Horace is not here mouthing some party line. It is a general and genuine belief. It runs through Livy, as, for example, when he complains of the neglect of the gods which afflicts his own generation (III, 20, 5) or urges that the observance of trivial religious matters had made Rome great (VI, 41, 8). It is the whole lesson to be learnt from the story of Camillus whose piety won the favour of the gods both for himself and for his country. It is prominent in Virgil also—in the *Georgics* at least as much as in the delineation of Aeneas' character in the *Aeneid*. The religious ideas expressed in his poetry are highly complex. Book VI, for instance, combines a wide range of traditional elements from Homer, Pindar and Plato together with the mystic idea of a descent to Hades, which we find described in fragments of Greek poetry or parodied in Aristophanes' *Frogs*, and fuses all these with specifically Roman beliefs and practices. The resulting vision would have puzzled most Romans. Nonetheless the final message is clear. The triumph of Rome is the triumph of religion.

It was this emotional atmosphere that Augustus was anxious to exploit, not cynically as Cicero would have done, who argued bluntly that 'gods are necessary to prevent chaos in society' (*On the nature of the gods* I, 3)—an idea summarised in Ovid's brilliant epigram *expedit esse deos et, ut expedit, esse putemus* ('the existence of gods is convenient and, as it is convenient, let us assume it'; *The Art of Love* I, 645)—but from a deep sense of mission. There was no idea in Augustus' mind that the Roman people should be drugged by the opiate of religion into torpid acceptance of his rule. The evidence rather indicates that he appreciated that the general mood could be harnessed and directed to give Rome a new start. His success is to be measured by the fact that Roman religion survived as a more or less vital force for another four hundred years and that Romans did recover their self-confidence. This could never have been achieved by some arbitrarily imposed 'religious revival'. What is much more important is to study the different ways which Augustus used to satisfy the widespread desire for religious fulfilment.

The first task was, of course, the simple one of reconstruction. Augustus' own words speak for themselves: 'I rebuilt in my sixth consulship [28 B.C.], on the authority of the Senate, eighty-two temples and overlooked none that needed repair' (*Res Gestae* XX, 4). But we know also that he made the sons or descendants, if they survived, of original dedicators of temples responsible for their upkeep and restoration (Dio LIII, 2, 4). By these means the fabric of the religious buildings at Rome was wholly renovated. It was part of the process of 'rebuilding Rome in marble' and it was a deserved tribute which Livy paid when he described Augustus as 'the founder and restorer of every temple' (IV, 20, 7). A corollary of this activity was, as we have seen, to fill the chief priesthoods and ensure that the religious machine was in good running order. It so happened that one of his main rivals, Lepidus, held the office of *pontifex maximus*, but a scrupulous regard for propriety prevented Augustus from deposing him (*Res Gestae* X, 2). Only on Lepidus' death in 12 B.C. was Augustus elected to the leading position of the hierarchy.

Mere buildings, however, will not revive religion. It is necessary also to awaken an interest in worship. The old gods were almost too familiar. Something new was needed to capture men's imagination. It would have been dangerous (and unlike Augustus) to have encouraged some of the new oriental cults, such as Isis or Mithras, which were already gaining in popularity among the mixed ethnic elements in the city. Instead, Augustus singles out for special devotion certain of the traditional gods who had been relatively dim up till now.

First of these was Apollo. 'Your Apollo now reigns,' Virgil sang in *Eclogue* 4, written in 40 B.C., long before Augustus' final victory. Indeed Augustus' respect for Apollo can be shown to be long-standing. He founded a temple of Apollo on the Palatine in 36 B.C. and later attached to it a superb library (Suetonius, *Augustus* XXIX, 3). Apollo, according to Propertius (IV, 6, 29*ff*.), appeared to him at a critical moment at the battle of Actium and ensured his success. Throughout Augustus' life he remained his favourite and patron god. Yet until then Apollo had not been of much note at Rome. He was almost exclusively a god of healing, as Livy records (IV, 25, 3). He was invoked as such by the Vestal Virgins (p. 29). But Augustus saw him as much more than that. He was for him the god of peace and civilisation, an appropriate deity to watch over the progress of

his new order. This was the character of the god which
Augustus tried to project. To Tibullus he becomes
'gentle Apollo' (II, 5, 79); to Horace he is the god who
will allow one to enjoy one's belongings in peace (*Odes*
I, 31, 17). Apollo epitomised everything that was new
and young—and successful.

Another deity to be promoted was Mars. Mars had
since time immemorial been a powerful force at Rome—
as the god of war and the god who guarded agriculture
from disease. He is invoked in the song of the Arval
Brethren; his altar had long stood in the Campus
Martius, the field named after him; a month bore his
name. But Augustus seems to have wanted to stress two
new aspects of the god. The first was that of Mars, the
father of Romulus, the progenitor of Rome. An inscription set up in the Forum under Augustus begins with
the proud claim: 'Romulus, son of Mars, founded Rome'
(*I.L.S.* 64).[1] It is well known that before he adopted the
title of Augustus he had toyed with the idea of calling
himself 'Romulus'. Secondly, however, it was in a special
capacity, as Avenger (*Ultor*), that Augustus revered
Mars. There was much to be avenged—not least the
murder of his adoptive father, Julius Caesar, and the
ignominies which Rome had suffered. As early as 42 B.C.
he had vowed a temple to Mars 'in vengeance of his
father' (Suetonius, *Augustus* XXIX, 2). Again in 20 B.C.
he ordered a temple of Mars Ultor to be built to com-
memorate the recovery of the standards captured by the
Parthians and he records in the *Res Gestae* XXI that it
was eventually dedicated in 2 B.C. The worship of Mars
Ultor was a convincing sign that Augustus intended to
put things to rights. As such, it is echoed in the poetry
of the period. Horace (*Odes* I, 2, written probably in
28 B.C.) dilates on the avenger of Caesar and Ovid (*Fasti*
V, 561*ff.*) glorifies the new cult. Nothing, however,
illustrates better the way in which Augustus wanted
Mars Ultor to inspire the Romans to triumph over their
past failures than the hopes which, according to Dio (LV,

[1] See footnote to page 12.

10, 2), he expressed in 2 B.C. at the dedication ceremony:
he and his grandsons would regularly visit the temple;
every youth, enrolling for the first time in the ranks of
the military, should pay his respects there; every com-
mander setting out on any expedition should make it his
starting point.

Apollo and Mars—gentle peace and just war. Here is
the same theme as the famous prophecy in Virgil's
Aeneid VI: 'Remember, Romans, that your role is to
impose the way of peace, to spare the humbled and to
beat down the proud.' The *Aeneid* also reveals a second
Augustan development. Ancient gods, by their very
nature and function, tended to be very localised: they
were gods who resided in or cared for particular places
or institutions (p. 29). It was difficult for a Florentine to
work up much enthusiasm for the patron god of Padua
or Naples, just as the god of corn-merchants had little
appeal for a silver-smith. There was need of a more
universal theology, a faith which would capture the
hearts of nations scattered from Britain to the Orontes.
In the end it was Christianity which succeeded, but
Augustus made deliberate efforts to meet the need. One
of the main consequences of the worship of the emperors,
as we shall see, was to provide a common focus of loyalty
and devotion. But, even before that was generally
accepted, there are clear signs of an attempt to univer-
salise Roman gods. They were to be the gods of *Italy*, not
just of Rome or Padua or Florence. In the *Aeneid* (VIII,
714) Virgil speaks of triumphant Augustus 'consecrating
an immortal vow to the *Italian* gods'. It is easy to forget
that the Social Wars in which Rome had to fight for survival against the rest of Italy (90 B.C.) were still a very
recent nightmare and that Italy was by no means a
united and homogeneous nation.

It is through poetry that so many of Augustus' ideas
circulated. Poetry articulates the thoughts of a generation, without the need for any conscious programme or
propaganda. The *Aeneid* and many of Horace's *Odes*,
especially the hymn which was commissioned for the
Secular Games of 17 B.C., put into words the thoughts

that were in people's minds and the interpretation of them which Augustus was anxious to foster. But there were other, visible media. There was a long tradition at Rome of using coin-types to convey political ideals. Coins, after all, are things which people handle and see every day. Augustus turned this tradition to his own purposes by stamping significant types on the coins which he minted from 27 B.C. onwards, such as 'Peace' and 'Victory'. In the same way, works of art, such as the golden shield dedicated on the Capitol, could be used to depict Augustan ideals. The Altar of Augustan Peace, dedicated in 13 B.C. (if, indeed, the surviving fragments do come from that monument), displayed scenes of religious processions as well as showing the arrival of Aeneas in Italy and the childhood of Romulus. These and many other sculptures will have kept the vision of a Rome that had grown great from small beginnings by cherishing the *pax deorum* constantly before the eyes of the common citizens. Some of this idealism will have penetrated their consciousness.

The finest expression of this new religious mood was the Secular Games of 17 B.C. There was a faint tradition that a hundred years was a span in the life of the world which should be marked by special religious ceremonies. There are traces of such celebrations as far back as 363 B.C. and 263 B.C., but the practice had lapsed in the late Republic, together with so much else. Now, however, various forces conspired to make people believe that a rebirth of the world was imminent, that a new *saeculum* was about to begin. It was partly the feeling that things *must* get better sooner or later, partly the influence of mystical ideas about the cyclical rebirth of souls, popularised by the great scholar, Varro, among others. There were numerous prophecies in circulation foretelling a new Golden Age, like the one uttered by Vulcanius when the comet appeared after Caesar's death in July 44 B.C. that it meant the end of the ninth century in the history of Rome and the beginning of the tenth, the century of the glorious Sun. The prophecies are echoed in Virgil's Fourth *Eclogue* (written in 40 B.C.) which alludes to the arrival of 'the lost age of the Cumaean prophecy'. Even more explicit is the reference in the *Aeneid* (VI, 789*ff.*) to Augustus Caesar 'who will found a golden age' (*aurea saecula*). It is against this background of hope that Augustus felt bold enough to stage the magnificent spectacle of the Secular Games in 17 B.C. and to commission Horace to write the principal hymn for it.

The actual records describing the details of the ceremony have survived on stone, so that it is possible to reconstruct in detail what happened. From 26 May, for three days, the population of Rome was issued with sulphur-torches for purifying themselves and their houses and was bidden to bring vegetable offerings to the *quindecimviri*. Then on three successive nights Augustus sacrificed publicly by the banks of Tiber to the Fates, to Eilithyia (the Greek goddess of childbirth) and to Mother Earth. By day he offered sacrifice to Jupiter Optimus Maximus on the Capitol, to Juno and, finally on the third day, to Apollo on the Palatine when Horace's *Hymn* was sung by a choir of twenty-seven boys and twenty-seven girls. The hymn unites the different strands of religious feeling which have been discussed above. Apollo is the central deity and the return of prosperity is confidently proclaimed in lines 57*ff*:

> Now Faith and Peace and Honour and ancient Morality
> And forsaken Virtue dare to return
> And Abundance is in evidence.

The great public sacrifices amid temples newly rebuilt and redecorated, accompanied by choral performances and sumptuous games, must have made a deep impression on the popular imagination. It did much to make the Golden Age seem a reality. The Happiness of the Era (*Felicitas Saeculi*) recurs as a theme on provincial inscriptions.

Peace, security, prosperity—these were the signs of the new age and they were blessings for which the emperor was directly responsible. The final stage in the renewal of Roman religion, in the reassurance that it really worked, came when the emperor himself was accepted as one of the gods. To modern minds this is a ludicrous idea. Indeed, it struck many Romans as pretty ridiculous, from Cicero's giggles about Julius Caesar's incipient divinity as 'Quirinus' tentmate' (*Letters to Atticus* XII, 45, 3) to Seneca's splendid Pumpkinification of Claudius, a parody on the supposed apotheosis of the emperor. But, in fact, in terms of Roman concepts, the notion was a perfectly serious and respectable one.

The Romans conceived of gods as powers who brought about the successful accomplishment of natural processes and human activities. To win a great victory, to restore order and prosperity to the world, to bring happiness to mankind were tasks which no man could perform by himself without divine assistance. Many notable Romans had believed that gods were personally associated with them. Julius Caesar, for instance, who claimed direct descent from Aeneas' son, Iulus, and hence from Venus, was, according to Dio (XLIII, 43, 3), 'absolutely devoted to her and was anxious to persuade everybody that he had received from her a kind of youthful radiance'. In gratitude for his successes, he dedicated a temple to Venus Genetrix in 46 B.C. and lavished on it a host of treasures. His dependence on Venus was so widely known that Cicero could jokingly refer to him in 49 B.C. as 'Venus' descendant' (*Venere prognatus*; *Letters to his friends* VIII, 15, 2). Similarly Pompey's son, Sex. Pompeius (who was admiral of the Roman navy for several years from 44 B.C.), believed himself to be the son of Neptune and dressed accordingly in a dark blue cloak (Dio XLVIII, 48, 5). Augustus himself, as we have seen, pledged his allegiance to Apollo.

It was one thing to believe that a god stood by your shoulder and helped you to overcome all your difficulties. It was only a short step from this to believe that you had within yourself divine powers. A god was someone who bestowed blessings, who made things work smoothly and well. If *you* could do this, you must be a god. It is this train of reasoning which led Lucretius to his noble encomium of Epicurus (5, 8–12):

He was a god, Memmius, a god
Who first discovered that principle of life
Which is now called wisdom and who by his art
Rescued human life from storms and darkness
And settled it in a clear, still light.

Exactly the same thought lies behind the acceptance of Christ by the African writer, Arnobius, in the third century A.D. 'Are we not then to regard Christ as a god and to give him the greatest worship paid to divinity that we can devise, since we have long received great blessings from him and await yet greater ones?' (*Against the pagans* I, 39). Above all, a god is a saviour. Yet there were many men who could legitimately claim to have saved more of their fellow-men than any god. The successors of Alexander the Great were regularly hailed as Saviours (σώτηρες) and the idea was by no means foreign in Republican Rome. Marius Gratidianus, praetor in 86 B.C., who carried out some popular currency reforms, was greeted with a spontaneous demonstration in which statues of him were set up throughout the city and honoured with incense and wine as a Saviour god. What was tolerated for an ephemeral benefactor like Gratidianus was a thousand times more justifiable in the case of a ruler like Augustus. Velleius Paterculus, an officer under Tiberius who turned to history in his retirement, eloquently captured the spirit of men's emotions at that time (II, 89): 'There was nothing that men could ask of gods, nothing that gods could offer to men, nothing that prayer could conceive of, nothing that ultimate bliss could achieve, which was not vouchsafed to the state, to the people, to the world by Augustus after his return to Rome.' There indeed was a man who gave gifts worthy of a god, as Propertius summed it up (IV, 6, 36)—*mundi servator*, Saviour of the World. To anyone who had lived during the fifties and forties the reversal of fortune which Augustus had brought about was a miracle, a true miracle. And it was an accepted fact in the ancient world, one which did much to forward the cause of Christianity in the early stages, that attested miracles

were proof of divinity. A character in Terence's *Brothers*
(535ff.) says, 'I make you a god in his eyes: I tell of your
miraculous achievements.' The reading public of the
late second century A.D. was familiar with popular works,
such as Philostratus' *Life of Apollonius of Tyana*, which
recorded the miracles of semi-divine heroes.

All of this aided the belief that the emperors were
more than human. In the East such a doctrine had long
been current. Alexander the Great had demanded and
secured recognition of his divinity ('If he wants to be a
god, let him be a god', the cynical Athenians are alleged
to have commented) and his successors used the status as
a support for their power and prestige. But even in the
Roman world the idea was not philosophically absurd.
We have seen that in popular superstition the soul was
regarded as enjoying a contingent immortality (p. 86)
and popular philosophy rationalised this by regarding
each soul as a portion of the great world-soul which it
rejoined at death. The greater the person, the larger and
purer the divine element inside him. Even Cicero who
indignantly protested that he 'could not be induced to
unite any man who has died with the religion of the
immortal gods', when a proposal to deify Caesar was
mooted (*Philippics* I, 13), had elsewhere admitted that
'there was no great man without some divine spirit' (*On
the nature of the gods* II, 167). Death only meant that
the divine spirit left its physical home and returned to
the world of gods, it might be, like Castor and Pollux or
Julius Caesar, as a new star in the constellation of
heaven. In one of his most religious works, the *Dream of
Scipio*, Cicero puts this idea quite clearly: 'To all who
have saved, helped or advanced their country, a fixed
place is assigned in heaven in which they shall enjoy
everlasting bliss.'

It is clear that Caesar, before his assassination, had
determined to claim divine status for himself. His
motives for so doing are not wholly clear. He may well
have felt that it would help to authenticate and justify
the absolute monarchy which he realised was the only
answer to Rome's perennial quarrels and disputes. In

1

May 45 his statue was set up in the temple of Quirinus
with the inscription 'To the Unconquered God'. Later,
statues were erected in temples throughout Italy; games
were established in his honour; the month of Quinctilis
was changed to July; finally, a temple to Caesar and his
Clemency was decreed and a special priest, of Divus
Julius, the first *flamen* to be created in the memory of
history, was appointed. His efforts to be divine were,
however, frustrated by death, but his example was
followed by Antony who posed as the New Dionysus. As
such he made a triumphal tour of the East in the years
from 41 B.C. onwards. In Ephesus 'women clothed as
Bacchants, and men and boys like Satyrs and Pans, led
the way before him, while the city echoed with pipes and
harps' (Plutarch, *Antony* 24). In Athens, he dressed himself as Dionysus and conducted day-long revels on the
Acropolis; when the Athenians unwisely flattered his
whim, by offering the goddess Athena to him in marriage, he accepted with alacrity and exacted a dowry of
£1,000,000 (Dio XLVIII, 39, 2). All this sounds bizarre,
but it should be remembered that Antony's sphere of
influence was the East and that Cleopatra, who as Queen
was reverenced in Egypt as a goddess, was his consort.

Augustus moved more circumspectly. He could see the
help which divine recognition would give both to the
re-establishment of the old religion and to the unifica-
tion of the Roman Empire, but he was deterred by the
lesson of Julius Caesar from pressing to be worshipped
as a god during his lifetime. Instead he reasserted the
divinity of Julius Caesar, consecrating a temple to him in
29 B.C. as a gesture that he was Caesar's legitimate successor and heir, and styling himself thereafter as *Divi filius*,
the Son of God, and as Augustus ('the reverend'). But the
desire of ordinary Romans to express their sense of
religious obligation to Augustus was too strong to be
overlooked and too socially beneficial to be disregarded.
Augustus encouraged two cults which fell a little short of
proclaiming his full divinity, but left the possibility that
he was indeed divine wide open for posterity to decide
after his death in the light of his achievements. The first

of these was the Divine Will of Augustus, the *Numen Augusti*, a cult in accord with the common belief of a divine spirit within man. It is first alluded to by Horace about 13 B.C. when he talks of founding altars where oaths may be taken 'by your *numen*' (*Letters* II, 1, 15). Similarly Ovid invites the reader 'to worship the *Numen Augusti* and duly to invoke the god' (*Tristia* III, 8, 13). Altars dedicated to the *Numen Augusti* dating from A.D. 12 (two years before his death) have been found in Gaul and in Africa and a special festival was inserted in the calendar for 17 January. The second cult, the Genius of Augustus, is more obscure. Originally the Genius seems to have been the procreative power that enables a family to continue generation after generation. Every house had the bed of its Genius (*lectus genialis*) in the main hall. As time passed, the Genius merged with a quite different idea, that of a personal *daemon* who watched over an individual throughout his life, a guardian angel. This is how, for instance, the later writers Censorinus and Apuleius defined it. The Genius was not a very promising idea in Roman religion. It served mainly to personalise the unity of the family, which is why slaves swore by their master's Genius. A few inscriptions suggest that Augustus allowed his Genius to be similarly invoked.

Conclusion

THE smoke no longer curls up from the sacrifices in the Forum; the augur no longer takes his seat on the Capitol to watch the birds wheeling overhead. Yet its ultimate failure should not tempt us to underestimate the validity of Roman religion. For over a thousand years it satisfied the spiritual urges of a wide range of peoples, because it offered an intelligent and dignified interpretation of how the world functions. The ultimate test of a religion is that it works; and the Romans truly believed that their religion worked. Otherwise Roman civilisation would have collapsed with Augustus. For the social and constitutional recovery which he engineered could not have succeeded unless it had been based on a widely diffused religious confidence to make it succeed. Such a confidence is not something which a statesman can artificially contrive. It springs from a spiritual awareness. Roman gods were so intimately involved with human activities that neither could thrive without the co-operation of the other.

Romans could, therefore, and did, claim that their religion was verified by history. True religion for them, as opposed to superstition, was 'to honour the gods fitly *in accordance with ancestral custom*' (Cornutus). It was a fine, yet tolerant, religion whose adherents committed very few crimes in its name and who were healthily free of neuroses. It failed because men's view of the world changed. There were new spiritual needs to be satisfied, needs which arose from the changed circumstances in which men lived, needs which philosophy and the religions of the East, above all Christianity, were more attuned to satisfy. Yet there is something deeply moving about the plea which one of its last champions, Symmachus, put forward: 'Everything is full of God. Whatever men worship, it can fairly be called one and the same. We all look up to the same stars; the same heaven is above us all; the same universe surrounds every one of us. What does it matter by what system of knowledge each one of us seeks the truth? It is not by one single path that we attain to so great a secret.'

List of Authors cited in the text

Aeschylus   525/4–456 B.C. Athenian tragedian.

Apuleius   Born about A.D. 123, in Africa. Pagan philosopher.

Arnobius   Wrote about A.D. 305 an attack on paganism. African.

Artemidorus   Wrote about A.D. 180 an interpretation of dreams. From Ephesus.

Athenaeus   Wrote an encyclopaedia in the form of a dinner-party conversation. About A.D. 200.

Augustine, St.   A.D. 354–430. Christian theologian.

Augustus =   C. Octavius. 63 B.C.–A.D. 14. Took the name Octavian in 43 B.C. and Augustus in 27 B.C. First Roman emperor. Wrote Autobiography (*Res Gestae*).

Cato =   M. Porcius Cato, the elder. 234–149 B.C. Statesman. Wrote a treatise on agriculture.

Catullus =   C. Valerius Catullus. *c.* 84–54 B.C. Poet.

Cicero =   M. Tullius Cicero. 106–43 B.C. Statesman. Wrote letters, speeches, philosophical treatises.

Dio =   Cassius Dio Cocceianus. *c.* A.D. 163–230. Historian.

Dionysius of Halicarnassus   *c.* 50–1 B.C. Historian.

Epictetus   *c.* A.D. 55–*c.* 135. Stoic philosopher. From Phrygia.

Festus =   Sext. Pompeius Festus. Wrote about 190 A.D. a dictionary.

Festus =   Rufius Festus. Wrote about 370 A.D. a history of Rome.

Gellius =   A. Gellius. *c.* A.D. 123–*c.* 163. Wrote an antiquarian encyclopaedia (*Noctes Atticae*).

Homer   *c.* 750 B.C. Epic poet.

Horace =   Q. Horatius Flaccus. 65–8 B.C. Poet. Wrote *Odes, Satires, Epistles.*

Juvenal =   D. Iunius Iuvenalis. *c.* A.D. 50–*c.* 127. Satiric poet.

Livy =   T. Livius. 64 B.C.–A.D. 12. Historian.

Lucan =   M. Annaeus Lucanus. A.D. 39–65. Wrote epic
                poem on Civil Wars.
Lucretius =   T. Lucretius Carus. c. 94–c. 55 B.C. Wrote
                didactic poem *De Rerum Natura* on the
                physical theories of Epicurus.
Macrobius =   Macrobius Ambrosius Theodosius. Lived
                about 430 A.D. Wrote a literary commentary
                on Virgil.
Martial =   M. Valerius Martialis. c. A.D. 40–c. 104. Poet.
Nepos =   Cornelius Nepos. c. 99–24 B.C. Biographer.
Nigidius =   P. Nigidius Figulus. Contemporary of Cicero.
                Wrote antiquarian works.
Ovid =   P. Ovidius Naso. 43 B.C.–A.D. 17. Poet.
Paul, St.   Died A.D. 66. Christian apostle.
Persius =   A. Persius Flaccus. A.D. 34–62. Satiric poet.
Petronius =   T. (or C.) Petronius Arbiter. Died A.D. 66.
                Novelist.
Philostratus = Flavius Philostratus. c. A.D. 170–248. Philo-
                sopher and biographer.
Plautus =   T. Maccius Plautus. c. 251–180 B.C. Comic poet.
Pliny the Elder = C. Plinius Secundus. A.D. 23–79. Wrote
                encyclopaedia.
Pliny the Younger = C. Plinius Caecilius Secundus, nephew
                of above. A.D. 61–113. Statesman. Published
                collection of letters.
Plutarch =   C. Mestrius Plutarchus. c. A.D. 46–c. 120. From
                Chaeronea in Greece. Wrote biographies and
                philosophical works.
Polybius   c. 203–c. 120 B.C. Greek historian.
Propertius =   Sext. Propertius. c. 50–c. 10 B.C. Poet.
Sallust =   C. Sallustius Crispus. 86–34 B.C. Historian.
Seneca =   L. Annaeus Seneca. 5 B.C.–A.D. 65. Statesman
                and philosopher.
Servius =   M. Servius Honoratus. Wrote about A.D. 390
                commentary on Virgil.
Statius =   P. Papinius Statius. c. A.D. 45–96. Poet.
Suetonius =   C. Suetonius Tranquillus. c. A.D. 69–c. 140.
                Biographer of emperors.
Symmachus =   Q. Aurelius Symmachus. c. A.D. 340–c. 402.
                Statesman and orator.

Tacitus =   P. (or C.) Cornelius Tacitus. *c.* A.D. 55–*c.* 117.
             Historian.
Terence =   P. Terentius Afer. *c.* 195–159 B.C. Comic poet.
Tibullus =   Albius Tibullus. *c.* 48 B.C.–19 B.C. Poet.
Valerius Maximus   Wrote about A.D. 31 an anecdotal history
             of Rome.
Varro =   M. Terentius Varro. 116–27 B.C. Scholar.
(C.) Velleius Paterculus   *c.* 19 B.C.–A.D. 35. Historian.
Virgil =   P. Virgilius Maro. 70–19 B.C. Poet.
Vettius Valens   Wrote about A.D. 150 on astronomy.

C.I.L. = *Corpus Inscriptionum Latinarum*
I.L.S. = *Inscriptiones Latinae Selectae*
             These are the two standard collections of Latin
             inscriptions.

Select Bibliography

ONLY works in English are given. The standard works of reference on Roman religion are in German: G. Wissowa, *Religion und Kultus der Römer*, Beck, Munich, Second Edition, 1912; K. Latte, *Röm. Religionsgeschichte*, 1960.

F. Altheim, *History of Roman Religion*, translated by H. Mattingly, Methuen, 1938; New York, Dutton, 1938. Contains much speculation about the early history of Roman religion but gives a good picture of the fusion of Greek and Roman culture.

H. J. Rose, *Ancient Roman Religion*, Hutchinson's University Library; New York, Hillary House Publishers, 1948. The best general introduction to the subject.

C. Bailey, *Phases in the Religion of Ancient Rome*, Oxford University Press, 1932. Readable.

W. Warde Fowler, *The Roman Festivals*, Macmillan, 1899. The only detailed account in English of the festivals of the Roman religious year. Out of date in some particulars.

W. Warde Fowler, *Religious Experiences of the Roman People*, Macmillan, 1922. An old and long book, full of interesting ideas.

L. R. Taylor, *The Divinity of the Roman Emperor*, Middletown, Connecticut, Monograph of the American Philological Association, 1931.

L. R. Taylor, *Party Politics in the Age of Caesar*, Sather Classical Lectures, Berkeley, University of California Press, 1949. Good account of the use and abuse of religion for political purposes.

A. D. Nock, *Conversion*, Oxford, Clarendon Press; New York, Oxford University Press, 1933. Traces the conflict of religion and philosophy in the ancient world and shows how the rise of Christianity was accompanied by the growth of religious intolerance.

R. Syme, *Roman Revolution*, Oxford, Clarendon Press; New York, Oxford University Press, 1939. The best account of the literary, social and historical developments at the end of the late Roman Republic.

F. Cumont, *After-life in Roman Paganism*, New Haven, Yale University Press, 1922.

Index

(a) Gods

131

(b) General

N.B. Personal names are listed under the form most familiar in English. Names of the emperors are given in capitals.